Building
Your Best Life

Bridget,
You are the creator
of your best life.

Love,
Grandma Sandy

Building
Your Best Life

A YOUNG PERSON'S GUIDE TO
Creating the Life You'd Love to Live

MERIE WEISMILLER WALLACE,
MFA, SMPSP, CBCP

ARCHWAY
PUBLISHING

Illustrations by Cassie Alisande Wallace
Cover photographs by Merie Weismiller Wallace
Author portrait photograph by Alexander Schottky

Archway Publishing books may be ordered through booksellers or by contacting:

Archway Publishing
1663 Liberty Drive
Bloomington, IN 47403
www.archwaypublishing.com
844-669-3957

Because of the dynamic nature of the Internet, any web addresses or
links contained in this book may have changed since publication and
may no longer be valid. The views expressed in this work are solely those
of the author and do not necessarily reflect the views of the publisher,
and the publisher hereby disclaims any responsibility for them.

ISBN: 978-1-6657-5431-6 (sc)
ISBN: 978-1-6657-5433-0 (hc)
ISBN: 978-1-6657-5432-3 (e)

Library of Congress Control Number: 2023923737

Print information available on the last page.

Archway Publishing rev. date: 09/18/2024

To my eighteen-year-old self, what no one ever told me.

To my innovative daughter.

To all the young people of the world. May you
actualize and meet your full potential.

Contents

Foreword

Congratulations! You are holding in your hands a life-changing book—one I wish I had had when I was younger. ***Building Your Best Life*** by Merie Weismiller Wallace is an inspirational and empowering exploration of your innate ability to create a healthy, meaningful and fulfilling life. While Merie mainly wrote it as a guide for teens and young adults, it is applicable to anyone at any age and any time when you are looking for direction in your life.

In a rapidly changing world where being inexperienced can seem daunting, this book serves to normalize the many concerns and questions you may have about what the future will bring.

Merie has had a very successful career as a still photographer in the film industry, and many of the iconic images you've seen are hers. Included in this book she shares what it took to achieve her success, and then she shows you how to personally customize it so you can follow your own unique path.

Taking concepts from many eras, cultures and strategies, and translating them into clear tips and tools for making personal choices, Merie lays the foundation for you to create a fulfilling future in *all* areas of your life, not just professional. Between the tools she describes in this book and the workbook she also offers, you will be empowered to take responsibility for building your own best life while enjoying the process.

If you are a young person, this book will help you bypass some of the more common mistakes most people make, and more easily take positive action toward creating your own rewarding future while at the same time contributing to the betterment of life on earth.

Here's to your success!

— Jack Canfield, *New York Times* bestselling author of *The Success Principles™: How to Get from Where You Are to Where You Want to Be* and the *Chicken Soup for the Soul®* series

Acknowledgments

Thank you to my support team during the process of creating this book:

Cassie Wallace for her thorough, scathing, applauding and detailed editorial work, and her serious push for objective integrity.

Georgia Sargeant, initial substantive editor.

Beta readers Tal Wallace, Jenny Newell, Jessica Keesler, Donna Pace, and Tawnee Hensel.

Partial beta readers Kimberly Hunn and Amanda DeMaria.

Mariana Chaffee, final read-through adviser.

Barbara Laing, Karen ZoBell, and Ellen Freund for their sincere and detailed support efforts.

Jack Canfield, Katheryn Trestain, and the 2021 Mastermind Group of friends, advocates, and accountability partners who encouraged me as I wrote the first draft.

Jack Canfield and Deborah King for their important support and focused dedication to the wellbeing and advancement of others.

The Archway Publishing team.

Emmet Sargeant and Beagle Sound Studio in Santa Barbara, California for the *Building Your Best Life* companion audio book recording and production.

Thanks to Tal Wallace for believing in me and supporting my efforts when I doubted myself as a young photographer, and again at the beta-draft stage of this book.

Introduction by the Author

I was a young person who didn't know what I wanted or what I could do with my life when I grew up. Like so many, I walked through schools and unskilled summer jobs reacting to what life presented. I saw others who seemed to know what they wanted, but I didn't know what I was good at or what mattered enough to me to pursue. I didn't have a clear idea of how I'd love my life to be. On the outside, I was happy and gregarious, yet inside I didn't have confidence in my abilities. I didn't know that my individuality and authenticity were strengths. I had no idea how to look for an interesting job, build a meaningful career, or why someone would want to hire me. I knew I'd have to work for a living, but I was a creative person trying to pour myself into a linear education and business model. I was a young woman who wanted a husband and children but not to be dependent or underactualized. Deep down, I felt like there must be more to life than what I was seeing around me in the rat races of competitive schools and scarce or harrying jobs.

So I started searching. I was driven to travel and adventure, to read books and take workshops, and to live in other cultures. I came across ideas and facts that no one had ever told me and practices I'd heard people put down because they didn't actually understand them. I picked and chose what made sense to me and *finally* started making authentic choices and meeting kindred spirits whose ideas astonished me and opened my eyes and mind.

The results are in this book.

Have you ever felt that you are unusual but trying to conform? Do you know what you want to do to support yourself financially—or with your life? Maybe you have an idea, but you're not sure how to get there. Are you among the many people just trying to handle your circumstances, sensing that there is more you want out of life than what seems available to you?

If you said yes to any of those questions, then this book is for you. You can explore it with the secret knowledge that it is one way to get where you belong. Let me support you on your path toward meaningful work, improving family dynamics, achieving personal growth, inspiration, and self-actualization—now and as you continue to grow through your years.

What you'll find on these pages has been drawn from many cultures and perspectives. Some ideas are obvious, others are obscure, some are counterculture, some are philosophical and spiritual, and some are misrepresented in Western culture but eye-opening. I want to empower you to make positive changes while strengthening the parts of your life that you already love. Like any good toolbox, this book is filled with diversity so that you can pick the right tools for your unique interests and circumstances.

You might be surprised to know how many people pick their heads up late in life and ask themselves, "How did I end up here?" and they begin a path of personal work to find themselves and their happiness. I'm giving you a heads-up and head start to make choices that will help you claim your life—starting young! *Building Your Best Life* will help you discover your authentic self and break through uncertainty. It will help you tip the scale toward new thinking so that you can bring value into your life.

May you become your authentic, inspired self, living happily in active support of a flourishing planet.

Enjoy the read, enjoy the process, and think for yourself.

Sincerely,
Merie Weismiller Wallace
www.BuildingYourBestLife.net

Chapter One

What No One Ever Told Me

Whatever you can do, or dream you can, begin it.
Boldness has genius, power and magic in it. Begin it now.

—Writer and scientist Johann Wolfgang von Goethe (1749–1832)

Y ou are not adrift in the sea of life. In the best way, your
life is up to you.

Right now, that may sound like freedom to you or like a
daunting responsibility. Either way, imagine that there are important
and exciting ways to actively build your life—one that you will love
to live and that will allow you to experience happiness and fulfillment
no matter where you are—starting today.

And *you* are the right person to do it for yourself.

This book holds concepts and methods I learned during the
adventure of my life, things that no one ever told me about: interests,
talents, imagination, choice, and intention, including truths I
definitely learned the hard way. It really started when I was failing
in junior high because I wasn't interested and didn't care, and one
day I imagined with displeasure where that was leading. Then I
imagined exactly what I would prefer, and through an odd series

of events, I found myself in a progressive and rigorous high school, which changed my life. No one told me I had used a technique of visualization that successful people use purposefully. No one was even talking about ideas like that for me to overhear. I never knew most of the ideas and techniques in this book existed, yet somehow I had a gut feeling that there was more to life than people were talking about in my early schools, jobs, and family.

I'm talking about things here and now in your life that you too can use to create a happy and fulfilling life.

Look around you. There are people who live their whole lives working jobs or staying in relationships they don't enjoy, simply reacting to what happens around them, overeating or drinking to relieve boredom or assuage pain, and not making their own choices. They live like anchorless ships adrift at sea, reacting to the winds, storms, and the doldrums of life.

Do you feel some longing or discontent with your life today, or with where it looks like you're headed?

If you start paying attention to what really matters to you, if you notice what comes your way and consider if it fits into what you want for yourself, and if you choose things that make you feel good, you can create a great life. Maybe you already know what you want to do for paid work, fun, interests, and to fix problems you notice. And maybe you don't. Either way, what you will discover in these chapters are ideas and techniques for building a life where you wake up happy, healthy, and fulfilled.

And the best part is that you can start from exactly the point in your life that you are at today, no matter what that seems like to you right now.

Sure, there will be ups and downs; that is a real part of life. But did you know that the down times are an important part of growing and learning to make important choices? Next time you are feeling low or irritable, ask yourself, "What would I do differently if I were in charge?" Imagine clearly how you would prefer things to be. It is a beginning, and there are tools throughout the book to keep you going. As you grow through ups and downs, rain or shine, being solid in yourself and in your balanced life will allow you to see the gold nuggets in your problems, handle the storms of life, and keep you sailing ahead on *your* authentic life course.

Many times when I was young, I experienced being a creative, unique soul trapped in a life where I felt powerless, reactive, and swept in directions I did not want to go and didn't belong. I felt it when I was memorizing facts in school, instead of understanding the remarkable life contexts they fit into. I felt it when advertisements glorified people and possessions I didn't have or couldn't relate to. As a teen, I experienced depression to dangerous depths, like when my boyfriend broke up with me and it hit me too hard (unknown to me, it was an echo from my childhood), and I thought my life was lonely and horrible. Yet I also knew deep down that something else was wrong that I just couldn't put my finger on. My problems were covered up and shoved down year after year, until one day, in my first year of college, struggling with an eating disorder and trying to study, something started to dawn on me "Wait a minute. On the outside, I'm gregarious and doing well in a good school. I have a great boyfriend. I have so much going for me. And at the same time, secretly I have bulimia, I feel blind and worried about my future, and I feel debilitating jealousy when my charming boyfriend shines around other people. Something is very wrong here." That is what started me on my journey out of the box.

I share that with you only to say that is where I started. Each one of us starts with our own problems and circumstances. It is what we do with them that matters.

Fast-forward to today, where, despite ups and downs, I have a family I love deeply, I love where I live, I have a remarkably successful and fulfilling career as a photographer (one that I surely didn't see coming!), and I'm certified in energy release work so that I can help other people in a way I find fascinating and rewarding. My life has not always been easy, and the path here wasn't clear, but it has been an exciting and remarkable journey. Using the tools I discovered along the way, I am happy now most days, and when I'm not, I can look at my turmoil for the truths about myself that I need to learn. I'm still on my path and persistent in my commitment to strengthen my life in all areas. I am not adrift in the sea of life. I am embracing my life as I develop my potential and enjoy the true alternatives available to us all. You can be engaged, fulfilled, and happy, too, starting from right where you are today.

Nobody spoke to me like this when I was young and starting out. No one ever told me what was possible. It seemed like they thought in another way, with cans and can'ts, shoulds and shouldn'ts; they saw the world in black and white. This book shares the tools and techniques I learned during my unexpected and remarkable life so that you can choose the ones that make sense to you and build your own life the way *you* would love it to be.

Don't Just Wait for Change

You might be surprised at how many people are simply waiting for their circumstances to change, waiting for a better day. They react to life as it comes, putting one foot in front of the other, and they do not have an awareness of what other possibilities are available at every moment. Or they think their situation is too difficult to get out of or that they don't actually deserve something better. Their burdens obscure their vision.

Yet there are many ways to think differently and change circumstances. For example, most young people probably assume that if all goes well for the next several years, they will end up with a steady job and a roof over their heads, right?

But what if *you* were to make *which* job and *which* roof your priority? What if you decided with certainty that you want a nice, affordable place to live in a town or district where you would really enjoy living? What if you had fun exploring where that might be and what kind of living situation suits you best? Maybe you'd like a dynamic apartment complex with a pool and gym, or a cool little private guesthouse with a beautiful backyard. Maybe you'd like to stay where you are and save money for an adventure. What would *you* choose? What would you *choose*?

Do you see how there is a difference in thinking? One is like a ship at the mercy of the winds, tides, and doldrums; the other is the course set by an active, interested person. And this is not just about your job and home; this is about every aspect of your life.

When I was in my late teens and early twenties, I had no idea what I wanted to be when I grew up. I knew I didn't want a boring and mundane job, but I didn't know what I could do to support myself that I'd be any good at or enjoy. I had no idea what my talents were; I wasn't aware of any skills or abilities. It was really stressful for me. I had a friend who clearly knew that she wanted to be a photojournalist, and every time she took a great picture or spoke with clarity about what newspapers and magazines she wanted to work for, I felt lost. I felt a strange longing, and I felt deficient. I didn't know what I wanted, I didn't know what I was good at, and I didn't have an interest I was focused on. That friend went on to have a great career in photojournalism, and I went on to have a different but equally successful career in photography as well, one that I did not see coming and had never even imagined existed! The point is I never needed to feel deficient. I never needed to suffer any self-doubt. I simply didn't know what was ahead.

It doesn't matter where you are today; clear or unclear, you can create a life that is meaningful to you. I didn't get where I am today by waiting for my circumstances to change or by simply reacting to life as it came. I got here by applying the principles I've written out in this book.

What No One Talks About

Nobody ever told me these things:

- A person can be as happy as they actively intend to be.
- Our thoughts are an actual force in our lives.
- We can set our intentions and affect the quality of our lives.
- If we work on our internal happiness and fulfillment, we will attract and discover circumstances, people, and things that work well for us.
- Almost everybody has personal problems as a result of stresses in their childhood, and they can heal these to become strong, centered, and cheerful people.
- When we repeatedly think negative thoughts and feel the associated negative emotions, neural pathways are created, and then it becomes a pattern to think and feel that way.
- When our mind or emotions are in that rut, there are effective things we can do to get out.

- People are subject to every law of nature, including natural laws as invisible as electromagnetic attraction, which govern us and can be used to our advantage.
- With or without religion, connected prayer has an energetic force and impact.
- Synchronicities are when life aligns similar energetic forces and frequencies.
- There are many options and many perspectives in life, not just singular "right" and "wrong."
- Every person is unique and has individual talents that, if cultivated, will bring us great joy and be of help to others.
- The health of our body is linked to the repeated thoughts and feelings we have.
- Repeated positive actions, thoughts, and emotions have long-term positive impact.
- The mind memorizes what you tell it is important.
- The feelings of joy and gratitude have energetic force and influence.
- Indecision brings mixed results.
- Everything that has ever been invented or created started with one imagined idea. Then persistence created the outcome.
- And the list goes on, with descriptions and explanations throughout the book!

Let Your Emotions Be a Guide

No one told me that if something makes a person feel good emotionally—genuine positive emotions like love, inspiration, gratitude, and joy—it is an important clue for personal direction, and that choosing what feels right is a tool for creating health and happiness. No one told me, but it's true. I'm not referring to pleasures or substance effects; I'm talking about honest, positive emotional reactions, like where something makes you happy or curious, cheerful or grateful!

Let's say that you are looking at a list of jobs or classes, and you see some you know you aren't interested in and others that look okay or interesting. If you pick the ones you think you'd enjoy (and the teacher or boss is good or supportive), you'll feel fulfilled and involved when you are there. But if you pick one you "should" take but aren't excited by, you will probably feel obligated rather than inspired when you are there. This is generally true, unless you end up with an amazing teacher or boss, or you purposefully set your intention to get the most out of your situation wherever you are.

Intention + Action = Results

Intention can be defined by its synonyms: advance planning, deliberateness, design, forethought. It is your intention to have a life where you are happy and fulfilled. This is not accidental success or reacting to circumstances. This is deliberately conceiving of your authentic life using your interests, talents, and what matters to you, intentionally designing your life with your creative aesthetic, and purposefully planning the steps on your path toward what will free you up to be happy.

Your intention in every situation is amazingly effective and is necessary to make things happen. Intention has to be linked to related action; otherwise, it is just like yearning, wishing, and wanting from your couch. The combination of intention, inspiration, and related action holds great creative power—as Goethe insightfully describes in the quote at the beginning of this chapter!

Repetitive Thoughts Are Self-Fulfilling

Did you know that repeated thoughts have a force in your life? Or did you just think, as I did, that thoughts come and go and are mostly harmless, annoying, and random? Not so, and this fact may be as invisible to us as the scientific laws governing internet, TV, and radio—but scientifically, it is true. Repetitive thoughts create neural pathways, which is part of how habits are formed and maintained (see appendix 2 for interesting books on how the brain works). There is a physical connection between our thoughts, feelings, and what happens in our lives and health. It's a simple fact: good thoughts and feelings—like reacting positively to an experience you enjoy or taking a minute to be grateful—have a positive effect on us, and repeated negative thoughts and feelings—like stress and sorrow reactions to repeated negative experiences—have a negative effect on our body, our greater outlook, and on the choices we make.

Let's say you can't stand something in your life, and you worry about it and dwell on that problem day after day. That dwelling becomes a neural pathway, a thought pattern, and pretty soon, you will spend more time suffering the problem than looking for solutions or finding what else you would prefer. Your mind literally starts to memorize being unhappy. Your mind memorizes what you tell it is important.

Here's another thing the mind does regarding dwelling on negatives. Have you ever been stressed, exhausted, or overwhelmed, and you start feeling low in your mind and drag yourself to where you have to go—and then you get a great night's sleep or two, and the same things or situations seem manageable? Good sleep promotes feelings of well-being. People wake feeling better physically and psychologically after a good night's sleep, and over time, worse without enough. So many people stay sleep deprived, exhausted, and stressed, and they stay believing that life is overwhelming and unbearable. They complain about how awful everything is. They get sick a lot and do not know why. They are sure they don't have any choice but to stay up late and set a loud alarm to get them up in the morning after too few hours of sleep. And they spend their days burdened by their problems, repeating negative thoughts and feelings, and often not doing as well at work or school as they could.

The fact is if you dwell on your problems, your mind memorizes that "this unfortunate thing" is factual and important to you, and your mind returns to it and notices it from then on. That's how the mind works. But the great news is if you acknowledge the problem and purposefully shift your thoughts and feelings to solutions, alternatives, or ways to resolve or correct it, the outcome of that thinking will be ideas for change, and your brain will memorize how important it is to create change and be happy. Show your mind what you want to be true. We each must work away from perspectives that focus on the problem and build or strengthen outlooks that focus on the specific solutions that make us feel good.

You are the architect of your life, and whether you act or react, intend or dwell, your thoughts and actions have force. Choose what you want to be true for you and put it into intentional, repetitive practice.

The Tools of Change

I'm not promising perfection; that isn't an option. This book presents tools and ideas that too many people don't know, for *you* to use as you purposefully create a life you're happy with, including tools that will help you get through or change life circumstances that don't feel good to you. You will explore how to make choices that become the foundation of a future full of the things that matter to you, including what you experience as success and well-being.

You will look at your life today, plan to keep what you love, improve what you don't, figure out what your skills and talents are, and plan things that will pay off now and later in happiness and fulfillment.

It's as simple and straightforward as the fact that if you love ice cream, and you keep thinking of ice cream, at a certain point you are probably going to go get some ice cream. Thinking about ice cream results in getting ice cream. If you don't care about ice cream and never think about it, you will almost certainly not make the effort to go get or accept ice cream. Generally speaking, no interest in ice cream generates no ice cream.

This principle is true in all areas of your life! The same goes for wanting a certain profession or training; if you think about it enough, if you intend to get it, you will create or find it or start to notice the path to getting it. If you don't, you won't. I hope it goes without saying that if you want something but refuse to do or can't do what is needed to obtain it, you won't get what you want. With interest and intention, perseverance, and taking necessary steps, an interest naturally generates a related outcome. Take the next indicated steps, and the path unfolds.

As a test, practice thinking about something small that you *honestly* want, like the solution to a problem, help with something difficult, or to get training in something that interests you. If you keep thinking positively, ingeniously, about that thing you want, your mind will memorize that it's important, and you will start to see leads to it; doors will open that you didn't notice before. Wonderfully, this is how life works.

Your Building Your Best Life &Workbook

At the end of each chapter, you'll find questions to explore in your *Building Your Best Life &Workbook*. Sometimes you will be listing ideas, and always you'll be encouraged to journal your reactions. This *&Workbook* will evoke realizations! It doesn't have to be perfect. It's okay to be spontaneous and quickly jot down what pops into your head, and it's okay to take your time and explore the ideas. If something seems difficult or ideas aren't coming to you, just move through areas of uncertainty with a basic, honest effort. You can always go back and add more answers if ideas come to you later, and I encourage you to! The point is always to tell your own story, your truth, not what someone else thinks you should do, even if your truth in the moment is "Wow. I have absolutely no idea!" Deep down, you know what you care about and what matters to you, what your interests are; they just may need some attention to become clear to you. They are important. When you are done, the process of writing your truths down and the resulting complete *&Workbook* will be 100 percent helpful to you.

And here's a challenge: try really getting inspired as you write in your *&Workbook*. When you purposefully feel connection, interest, or excitement as you tell your truth, it turbocharges your results! Sometimes, looking at ourselves can be difficult, so just do your best and be honest. As you write, write about now, what you think and feel at the moment you are writing. Remember, at all times, *you* are in control of this journey. This is *your* life. You are the captain of this remarkable ship.

Why No One Told You

So why is no one, or almost no one, talking about you being happy and intentionally planning a wonderful future?

The simplest explanation is that the people in your life think and talk about the things that are normal in your neighborhood, in your culture, and in the local religion—and frankly, many people are living in social and cultural bubbles that don't include other ways of thinking.

Even though many of these ideas are not being taught in the mainstream, that doesn't make them any less true. Science teaches some things, and religions teach other things. They often disagree, and some people want nothing to do with either, so they miss the gold nuggets in both. Other people stick to following existing ideas because they are familiar or feel safer than change. Depending on how you were raised, that's what you've been taught or overheard—until now.

Whether or not you already know what you want to do with your life, you will discover many interesting ways to open the doors for the tomorrow you would love to live. These ideas, tools, and techniques are both miraculous and ordinary. They open minds and doors and will set you up for success and fulfillment in all areas of your life.

That's a key: happiness and fulfillment are not stable possibilities if they are only in one part of your life and not in others. If you've got a wonderful place to live and you have roommates or family there, but everyone is constantly fighting, you won't be happy there! If you are all work and no play or no love, after a while, you will feel dry and unactualized. Happiness comes when all parts of your life are cared for and flourishing in ways that feel good to you.

So let's explore what is working for you now and what isn't, and build the plan and foundation for what *you* consider a happy life.

What's Working for You and What Isn't

In his book and related YouTube videos called *The Honeymoon Effect*, cellular biologist Bruce Lipton, PhD, explains that we learn openly and unconditionally until about the age of seven. What we experience in those years comes automatically with acceptance, and this acceptance of situations ultimately forms our beliefs as adults, for better and for worse. We may not like something that is happening, but we accept that it is so. In some cases, we'd do best to unlearn them! If we don't, we have a built-in tendency to repeat our parents', teachers', and caregivers' mistakes. This is true for everybody. Most of our personal baggage comes from our early lives. The good news is we can be at the helm of working out these problems and moving past learned perspectives and behaviors that are holding us back now.

The truth is you are the only person who can change your life for the best, and *you* are the perfect person to do it. You have everything you need inside you already; you just need to find and practice it.

Interest Is the First Step

If you have read this far, you're interested in creating a meaningful and happy life or shifting something in your life that isn't working for you. Perhaps you dream of living an adventurous life! Your interest is the first step. You have started. Or maybe you have no idea what you want to do with your life to earn money or express yourself creatively, and not knowing is bothering you. You have already begun the path of change. All that is needed is that you do what feels right to you, even if it's sometimes imperfect. Don't worry about mistakes along the way; they help us know what we *don't* want, which helps clarify what we do! Doing your best in any given situation is all you can do, and it has attractive energy and momentum.

Maybe you don't know what you want to do for fun, study, or work, but you know what you don't want. That's a great place to start! Or maybe your health or some physicality is bothering you. Maybe your family or the friends you spend time with now are rubbing you the wrong way, or they have possessions or talents you don't. In these chapters, you will gain tools and techniques to have what you enjoy, to enjoy what you have, and explore ideas that are meaningful for you.

The bottom line is feeling happy and fulfilled is physically and mentally good for you and those around you. If you need to work, why not love your job? If you live with people, why not enjoy them and still have space when you need it? Why not help your body be as healthy as it can be and create a balanced life with happiness and well-being as the normal, usual way you feel? All you have to do is your best in this process, and the outcome will be gratifying and something to be proud of, which will make you happy too!

The Goal of Happiness

Why do I keep emphasizing happiness? Because it's a high-frequency emotion, it feels good, and it's part of well-being. Yes, contentment and fulfillment are every bit as important as happiness, as are gratitude, love, grace, and peace of mind. So for the sake of this journey, where you are building your life in a way that makes sense to you, strive for what is important to *you*. It could be loving life, feeling joy, enjoying friendship, having adventures, being grateful, feeling compassion, or being of service. They're all great! I emphasize happiness throughout the book because when we choose things that make us feel good and fulfilled, when we reduce stress and negativity, then happiness and joy result naturally. Happiness is a natural expression. Happiness is our inner light. It's the smile that comes when we feel good, our natural condition in the absence of problems and blocks. Look at little kids playing or painting. They aren't worrying about something else; they are happy in the moment, loving what they are doing. So consider happiness as a natural goal, and see how much is encompassed and achieved in the process!

Open Your Mind to the Possibilities

Generally speaking, if you keep doing exactly what you are doing now, you will keep having the same results as you have now. It's true of circumstances and relationships. You can wait for things to change, or you can create change.

So this is a good place to start, where you are, to consider the results you would like to have. Not sure what that might look like? Open yourself up to new opportunities, try something different, choose the thing you normally avoid, say yes to something you have never done, or go somewhere you have never been just to explore the unknown. Take a dance class or buy a book on cheeses of the world! Spend the weekend in a town you've heard people talk about. Read the flyers on a local bulletin board and decide to do one thing you resonate with. When you do something new, experiences and opportunities open up that you never considered or knew existed. It's all information on your way to filling your days with things that matter to you!

The biggest example that I can think of in my life is when I was pre-med in college, and it was starting to dawn on me that it wasn't the right fit. That created great stress and worry because I was already invested with time, money, and pride. Not only that, but if pre-med wasn't right, then I didn't know what major or career was! Should I stay with the plan or follow my instincts? After great consideration, I signed up for a junior year abroad program in France, taking only exciting arts-related classes. I knew that when the semester was over, I'd be refreshed and ready to commit to the sciences, or I'd be clear I didn't want to! That was a large-scale experiment, but the principle works for small decisions as well. The purpose is to find what is best for you long-term, so take some small risks and opportunities, or large ones, as long as the choices feel good to *you.*

Do you know people who have routines that are ruts, not joys? Most people live in routines, whether they are happy or not, but it doesn't have to be that way. You can create routines and schedules that bring you fulfillment—or break out of routine and enjoy spontaneity.

Start by paying closer attention to how you react to situations and how you feel. If something makes you get excited, or laugh, or want to know more, or want to do it again, there is power in it for *you.* And if something threatens or scares you, take a minute to look at what that fear is. If something gives you a bad feeling, it may be in conflict with your true nature; or even if it's not bad, it may not be right for you.

As you begin this work, the things that you are planning on and preparing for—things that make you happy—will start to show up. Or maybe they have been there all along, and you will suddenly notice them, as if for the first time. This is the process of healing and strengthening in action, the results of making personal choices in process and effect.

What Seems Right to You?

Feelings like happiness and joy, naturally positive reactions, are indicators that what is happening is right for you.

For example, can you think of people you've met who just make you feel good whenever you're with them? There is more to that than meets the eye. It's not a chance meeting; it is an opportunity for well-being. What if you only had time to socialize one or two hours a day, and you spent it with friends who always complained or blamed? Conversely, what if you actively sought out people who make you laugh and share your interests in fun, and you spent those hours with them? It's a no-brainer; go with the folks you like, and you'll have a better week. And yet many people stay in the relationships that have come their way, never realizing that they could have actively chosen and created other relationships that would make them happy.

Consider, in everything that comes up, what seems right to you? What actually interests you? What do you care about? What matters to you? You know some of those answers already.

If you want to shift your life right now, or to figure out something like how you are going to love your paid job in the future, or how to fix something, the key is to pursue what you are interested in and would love to do at work and play. This is about checking in with yourself and acting on your preferences. Small steps toward these will open doors that you can't foresee, doors that lead to where you will love to go, or choose to go, on the way to loving your life.

The Satisfaction Is in the Process

This is a process of getting back to or becoming who you really are.

Look at other people. Some seem genuinely cheerful and at ease, some seem oddly neutral, and others seem always worried or annoyed. Most people who are genuinely happy have made some good choices to be that way, and often they've resolved some personal problems and are experiencing the benefits of that. We all can, and it's important to. Emotional, mental, and physical health are all equally important to your well-being and happiness.

You might think that you will be happy if you have more money. But you know there are plenty of people who have money who aren't happy. Wealthy people have as many family problems as poorer people, and the challenging responsibilities connected to managing money and property can be immensely stressful. So it isn't just money you need. We are looking at creating your life so that your time is filled with meaningful activities and relationships.

Or you might think someone is lucky and happy because of how they look. Yet there are plenty of people who look like that and are hiding deep unhappiness, and there are plenty of people who don't look like that and are happy.

So if it isn't money and appearances, what is it that creates happiness and contentment? In most normal situations, happiness is caused by feeling good about what is happening, not a result of reacting to circumstances. An elderly friend of mine recently told me, "If you have a clear intention and you have determination, you'll be fine!" I never heard that growing up, and it's powerful information to live by.

Your clear intention must be about something good that truly matters to *you* personally. This could be about clearing your relationship with a family member, wanting to learn an amazing activity, or finding training in something you want to do to support yourself financially. It's making a choice that feels right to you, holding it in mind, and making more choices that support it. Determination is persistence and keeping your eyes open for every opportunity that comes your way or that you can create. And you'll be fine because clear intention and persistence are the ingredients for success, as you'll see in future chapters!

Life's ups and downs will come to you whether you live small and fearful, sure and steady, or big and bold. If you take the steps, you can build a life, create a life, filled with the elements of happiness for *you.* If you are mostly happy, when life takes a turn, you will have the strength and balance to weather the storm. You can capture your days and come to enjoy the process along the way. The process is your life.

Life's Ups and Downs

I want to take a moment to acknowledge serious adversities like wars, car wrecks, natural disasters, and personal-level disasters like clinical depression in yourself or family, the consequences of living with alcoholism, a predator, a school bully, or a mean teacher or family member. These and other negative realities exist, and there is more in later chapters about coping with personal challenges, as well as some resources in appendix 1. In the face of adversity, our ultimate goal is to come through our unknowns, our struggles and traumas, being honest with ourselves about what has happened and is happening, and creating the life path forward with the most kindness, compassion, respect, empathy, and care for ourselves and others imaginable.

Life happens. It is how we respond that makes the difference in the quality of our lives.

With problems and adversities, there is no benefit in reliving blame, fault, or shame. Those viewpoints and emotions can be as self-perpetuating, toxic, and dangerous as the problem itself and can prevent you from claiming your power and agency. If you continually blame a teacher, parent, boss, ex, or anyone else for a problem that took place, that doesn't solve the problem; instead, it's like you have settled for their choices and are resigned to being upset! Yes, it's important to see the truth in the situation and to understand and name the other person's negative behavior—and then that's done, and it's your responsibility to figure out what you want to be different and how you can achieve it. And if a problem is directly caused by the choices of another person, it is important to get help and speak your truth in safe and constructive contexts to prevent the problems from repeating.

This is about honoring what is true for you, going forward purposefully from here, and revealing where your strengths and powers lie.

Onward!

Are you ready to sail your own ship on a course that feels right to you? In the next chapters, we'll identify what you enjoy most about your life today, what isn't working for you, and where some worrisome uncertainties lie. We'll use the results to design the course chart and steps for a future you're excited about!

Enjoy the process. This is all about you and what you'd love to have happen!

> *On the inside cover of your ♣Workbook, somewhere, in a*
> *size and color you like, write today's great date and maybe*
> *a design, doodle, or drawing using a good colored ink.*

✤*W*✤

✤*Workbook Exercises for Chapter 1*

Now to start your ✤*Workbook*! Take this time to write about you. Tell it like it is. Speak your truths, pull no punches, daydream, and imagine! If you don't have an answer, write that down, then journal a little to explore why it might be that you don't know. As you fill out your ✤*Workbook* pages, your story and game plan will emerge. This is one of the tools I alluded to, and we will use your truths to create your personal plan!

Open the ✤*Workbook* and fill out pages 1–3:

In the ✤*Workbook*, on page 1, you'll answer these questions: What would you change or add to your life today to make it better? What's missing? List everything that you'd like to change or improve, things that would make your life better for *you* personally.

In the ✤*Workbook*, on page 2, you'll make a list of what makes you happy. Ignite your dreams here! Anything! Things like specific music, favorite foods, a person, a pet, an activity, a hobby, what you *wish* was your hobby, specific beautiful places, specific nice people, your favorite room in the house, your favorite pen, sport, activity, and so on. No limits to great feelings here!

In the ✤*Workbook*, on page 3, you'll write out some statements about yourself. This is your home base. This is what makes you *you*. It includes some things that make you unique or different, and in this zone, different is great! They can be little things or big parts of you. All in!

Chapter Two

Starting Where You Are

The biggest impediments to realizing the
successes of which we dream are the limitations
programmed into the subconscious mind.

—Bruce H. Lipton, PhD, *The Biology of Belief*

A ll your experiences, thoughts, and actions have led you to
where you are now.

That's obvious, but do you see the significance? Your willing
or unwilling and passive or active participation in the experiences of
your life led to who you are and what you are doing today.

If you had willingly, unwillingly, passively, or actively participated
in going to the backyard just now, you would be in the backyard
right now. If you had been worrying or stressing or blaming just
now, you would be upset and unhappy right now. If you want out of
the backyard now, you have to leave and go to a place you'd rather
be or start working on a solution of how to leave. If you don't want
to be upset, you must purposefully take your thoughts and feelings
to a place you'd rather be. This is true for all of us. In fact, it is our
job and responsibility. If you remain reactive and upset when life's
inconveniences and discords happen, you will become increasingly

unhappy. Many people do, not knowing they have a choice. You can avoid that.

Look around you. So many people stay upset or unhappy with their lives, as if it's their lot in life, their only option. It's as if "My life is bad, and I'm unhappy" is a fact rather than a low time or a perspective. A more constructive description might be, "When something bad happens, I notice it, I decide not to dwell on it, and I purposefully focus my attention on the solution or on doing something else that is constructive and makes me feel good, like going on a bike ride or playing great music." It's the same situation with two different perspectives, reactions, and outcomes. Which outcome would you choose?

Five Steps to Assist Change

To start creating your meaningful, happy life, you don't have to wait for someone or something else to change.

People think they need to wait until they find a certain job or partner, or for something they want to happen. They wait for things to change when they are older, or they wait for a parent or friend to stop doing something annoying, or they plan on moving to a different town when they can. Those can help, but I advise you not to wait for change. There are many things you can start doing today—plans you can make, steps you can take, views you can shift—that will lead you to the life of your dreams. *Your* dreams, not someone else's.

Here is one five-step guide to acknowledging and shifting current problems or stresses:

1. *Notice it* (the old thinking, behavior, or reaction).
2. *Acknowledge it* (the old thinking, behavior, or reaction).

3. *Replace it* (with the new idea, behavior, or action).

4. *Feel great about that* (the new idea, behavior, or action).

5. *Move on* (with what is happening in the present).

If you feel like something you are doing isn't getting the results you want, those steps can help begin a shift. Let's say you have an irritable coworker, sibling, or parent, and when they are short-tempered or impolite, you feel the same way towards them and react by talking back or feeling furious. That's fairly normal; it happens all the time. But it is self-perpetuating and doesn't help the problem go away. The first thing would be to notice your reaction—notice you're upset—and for that moment, don't act on it. Acknowledge that you feel put out and disrespected. Then decide that, regardless, you are not going to act like they do; you're not going to talk back or go off and stew. In that moment, decide if you want to be silent and just watch them behaving badly, or to calmly point out that they have lost their patience, or in that moment, plan to find someone to support you. Choose something that feels right to you in the given situation, and then feel good about the fact that you didn't just react back! Next, as soon as possible, let the incident go and move on with whatever you were doing before it happened or what needs to be done now. Let it go so that you can get back to you. If you need to bring it to someone else's attention or theirs later, you can, but for the moment, don't react back, stew, or dwell. You made a different choice, so feel good that you did things differently, and keep going forward with *your* day.

Maybe today there are things in your life that don't feel right, things you wouldn't choose for yourself. This is true for everyone, but there is no need to be resigned to it. Often, looking at how you got where you are helps you make decisions about going forward. Read that again and put your mind to it. What led up to things going wrong?

The Way It Was

Maybe you have had a charmed life, or maybe unfortunate things happened that have stayed with you. Maybe both.

Realize that deep down you are not what happened in your past. Your past has influenced you, but your authentic self is still at your center. That is the self you can call on. That is the self where your stability and wisdom lie. Look at what you don't like or don't want about yourself or in your life and use it specifically to ask yourself, "What do I want to be different? What would a great difference look like for me personally?' In the *Workbook*, you'll be exploring these ideas, as they are the building blocks for change.

Take a Break

You know that if you feel bad about something and then go see a funny movie or spend time with people or animals you love, you end up feeling better. That's how the heart and mind work: they can shift gears and take a break or move beyond a problem. You can purposefully use that same technique of choosing meaningful things that you enjoy to shift out of being unhappy about difficult things in your life. With a clear mind, you can then decide on steps away from what isn't working for you and toward what is. We will explore that in your *Workbook*, and you can do it daily. This isn't about putting a small bandage on a deep cut or ignoring a problem, hoping it will go away. This is about breaking the cycle of dwelling on or being resigned to our problems or believing early-life programming as if it is a nonadjustable fact.

Obviously, if something is hurting you, you don't want to shift out of disliking it; you want to remove yourself or resolve the problem.

But generally speaking, this is about getting to clear waters where you belong, and not resigning yourself to cycling in any problem. This is about choosing situations that feel right to you as part of moving away from things that aren't, like negative friends, blame and shame throwers, boredom, or an apartment or job you can't stand.

Our Thoughts Are a Force in Our Lives

Our thoughts and intentions are actual forces in our lives, and you can use that force to build your life. Please understand that negative thoughts like engaging in self-criticism, blaming and shaming, and ruminating resentfully or angrily (and so on) are all bad for your physical and emotional health and your future. Whereas, being purposefully constructive and caring is good for your health and well-being; it, too, creates neural pathways you slip into—but for the good! Make every effort to catch negative self-talk and speech. Negative thoughts have negative impact.

One-sided positivity and communicating positively in negative situations are not the same as centered and grounded thinking, feeling, and speaking. There are established philosophies and practices, including Taoism and Dr. John Demartini's teachings, that explain how life (and the natural state of our universe) will always try to balance itself. If you purposefully speak and think with excess positivity, it will attract its balance in negativity; excessive yin will always attract matching yang. Opposites attract to create balance. We are not looking for an excess in anything (not even excessive good, which sounds great but is unsustainable and can attract negative balancing by irritated people who then push back). The objective is emotional and relationship balance.

For example, if someone speaks to you with excessive anger,

you may react oppositely with upset and recoil and go silent. Or, like attracting like, if they speak rudely, you may reactively speak in the same tone. You can try purposefully saying something positive in an effort to balance or diffuse their anger. But a fourth and most constructive response is staying calm and grounded, honoring your feelings about how they are speaking to you, and replying in an even manner—which is different from being positive and pretending everything is okay, which sadly often allows the other person to continue behaving destructively.

Our intention to honor our own feelings, while remaining calm and communicating truthfully, creates a force that affects adverse situations positively and has a great chance of effecting change. Our intention to catch negative self-talk and communication, and come from truth, is a force for change toward well-being.

An Important Tip: Be Nice

For the happy life you are creating, plan on being nice, kind, and easygoing.

Wouldn't that actually feel great? Again, this is not positivity; it's kindness and cheer. Hold it as an intention. In time, that intention will make all the difference in the world for your quality of life in everything you do. Don't underestimate its power. You can create a life with satisfying constructive relationships and activities, and being nice and respectful makes all the difference in sustaining it.

Here is an example from my life: In both fifth and sixth grades, I was the new kid in school who seemed weird to students and teachers. I was bad at sports and was among the last to be picked on teams. I had simple clothes in a wealthy district. I wanted to be liked and to make friends, so it was terrible, and I wasn't happy. I tried to fit in, but the years were a struggle. Then, before seventh grade and a new junior high, I had a fabulous and active summer. I was healthy and radiating happiness as I entered seventh grade. Suddenly, I was getting a shocking amount of positive attention. People smiled at me in the hall and sat next to me in class. I wasn't used to it! It felt great! In retrospect, the best part about it was that because I had experienced the opposite, I was grateful, and it gave me humility. Starting in seventh grade, I was always thankful for any kindness or popularity. I have remained nice and friendly toward others because I remember what it was like when people weren't nice to me, and it has served me my whole life.

In contrast, I had a friend who was always manipulating the people around her. She would be nice, and right when I trusted her, she would embarrass me with a belittling comment if I needed to wash my hair or ate more of something than a dieting person would. She was subtly masterful at manipulating, and it came across as powerful, almost charismatic. But in the end, of course the friend group fell apart. We couldn't take it, and she had to find a new entourage. People like that are hard to be around, hard to relate to, and hard to work with. In my field of work, there are notorious verbally abusive taskmaster bosses who burn their way through great employees, barely retaining the ones who stay because they flat-out need the money. And there are amazing and empowering bosses who attract the best employees, elicit their best work, and have great people clamoring to get on their projects!

My point is, through thick and thin, keep your act together. Choose to be nice and kind. Put icing on it by treating people with respect and empowering them to be their best selves and do their best work. Imagine the life you'd love to live. Wouldn't it be that way?

Self-Awareness Is Key

It's super important to notice what you do and don't like. You deserve that! And along with that, please notice if you are experiencing self-pity, irritability, or arrogance—which can creep in! They don't serve you well. If you feel them, notice it, acknowledge it, and then move on to feeling grateful for something nice or do something else that feels genuinely good. Change the channel.

Life, reactions, and emotions can get overwhelming at times, and all your feelings are 100 percent legitimate. There is no blame, shame, or thinking that you should be responding differently than you do. The thing is we need to learn to process our experiences, let go of repeat responses that don't make us feel good, and move away from situations that make us feel bad. So as you read on, if I encourage you to move away from an emotion or a negative reaction, please know that I am not finding fault; I bring it up because it doesn't bring happiness or well-being, and I am in full support of you growing and healing into grounded happiness. Everyone has negative reactions to things we don't like! They are important guides. The goal is not to live feeling badly but to grow past the reactivity and overwhelm to your grounded, processing, objective, and authentic self! That is the core of all of us, and it is within our ability to develop and maintain.

What Is Unacceptable? What Is Acceptance?

An important thing to learn on this path is the difference between accepting and acceptance.

Acceptance in this context does not mean compliance, cooperation, complicity, or agreement with something. By that definition, you do not have to *accept* what is happening if you don't like it. But healthy acceptance of a situation in the present means you see it for what it really is, you accept that it is what it is, whether you like it or you don't, and you are honest about how you feel about it. If there is something in your life that you don't like right now, see it and accept it for what it really is, so that you can figure out how to change your circumstances. Be honest. Call their behavior and your reactions what they really are. Is it dismissiveness or self-doubt? Name it and acknowledge that it is happening. It is amazing how powerful this is. So, for example, if you are insecure, fearful, or bad-tempered—or if one of your parents or a boss is—recognize it in the present and accept that it is happening. Accept that you don't like it. Don't make excuses for it like "I'm having a bad day." Hold no judgment and cast no blame; just hold honest acknowledgment.

And then decide that you don't need to settle for just wishing it was different, constantly comparing it to what you wish was true. Know that you can find or create an alternative, and this book has many tools to help you with that. Maybe you are in a toxic work or family relationship. Simply admit to yourself that it's not a good fit. Look at the details of what isn't working for you, and look at other relationships that are positive and healthy, noticing what the differences are. Then, instead of wishing yours was different, make it different if you can, or get support and create a sustainable plan to step out otherwise. If that's hard to figure out, you need more support and more information.

Maybe you don't have enough money to do what you want. Instead of wishing you did, figure out how much it will cost, see if there are grants or work programs, and open a dedicated savings account with your eye on the prize. Whatever you wish were true, instead of wishing, create a plan for that change for the better in your life.

Since you have personal problems (we all do), your action toward change is to acknowledge each problem as it arises, accept that it is the case now, start brainstorming alternatives that make you feel good, and break those alternatives down into a plan. That plan is what the ✒️*Workbook* is for. The plan will arise from the truths you write! You can do this. It's universal. Anyone can. It's normal ... even if we don't see many or any people around us doing it yet.

You Are What You Think

For better and for worse, what you are thinking and doing, participating in now, is setting up what will happen next. For example, as long as you are caring for your own needs and boundaries, if you are helping people wholeheartedly, doing good, the outcome will include positive results for you and others. If you are tolerating a toxic job or relationship, you will continue to have a toxic job or relationship. So catch yourself. Notice your life and relationships for yourself, accept things as they really are, and if your circumstances are not what feels good or right to you, focus your intentions on what you want instead.

What feels right to you is important, what makes sense to you is important, and what matters to you is important. How can we live satisfying and meaningful lives if we are reactively fitting into circumstances that are right for others but not for us? And what if the perfect situation for you is out there now, or you could create it, but you don't have time because you are so busy doing small things you don't enjoy? Whatever your choices are, whatever decisions you have to make, really consider how they make you feel. Choose the things that seem good to you.

By taking the time to do that, you are beginning. By taking steps to get what you want or learn more about it, you are calling in related circumstances that will begin to arise.

Claiming Your Happiness

Perhaps you don't know what to call in, you don't know what you want, or you don't know what to do next. Maybe you don't know what matters to you or what you're good at. Well, start by answering this question: what would make you happy?

Would you be happy working with a team of people hanging beautiful artisan wallpaper for good pay, and then going out after work some nights in a local darts league? Would you be happy sitting in your peaceful home with your cats and a cup of tea and editing books like this one online? Would you be happy working in a bustling office in a cool downtown district, working IT or in accounting for a conservation firm that supports your favorite cause? Would you be happy teaming up with a partner, where you run the house and kids and they work at the job of their personal dreams? Gauge what you might work at by how it makes you feel. Try gauging what school or training program is best for you by where your abilities lie. Try picking work, school, or volunteer time by what good cause you care about. Imagine—what would make you happy?

By naming the things that make you happy, you are claiming your happiness. Reread and purposefully do something on your Happy List from the ❧*Workbook*, page 2. Take steps toward what you do want, toward what makes you feel good. And next time a toxic situation arises, create a new thinking pattern. *No thank you. That doesn't work for me.* Say it out loud if it's safe and appropriate, or just say it to yourself and remove yourself if needed, or begin to figure out how to avoid it in the future. This is about acknowledging what you don't like and purposefully spending time on the solution!

You Are More Than Your Circumstances

No matter where you came from, who your family is, or how your health is, you are more than that. You are more than your circumstances. You are more than the situations that brought you to where you are today. We start with clear energy as children, and then as life happens around us (mostly with our grown-ups on their own paths), we experience things too hard or confusing for us to process. Without proper support and help, we can begin to harden. We create emotional armor to protect ourselves, especially if we are too young to create change. It happens to us all to some degree. It's part of life. Yet today, you don't want to keep that armor if you don't still need it. You want to move back to the clear energy of your childhood, onward to the person you are deep down, to recovering or discovering your authentic self. And you can. We all can, and we are happier in our lives when we do.

The difference will be that you become stronger and wiser for having experienced your particular ups and downs. So if your personal blueprint was musical, but you haven't been involved with music for years, you are still musical, and all you have to do is reclaim what interests you and matters to you. If you were intuitive, if you were funny, if you loved nature, it's all still there! Your authentic self is still there, and you are simply more experienced, not a different person.

So Who Are You Anyway?

Let's take a look at you for a moment. Who are you anyway? Actually, deep down, authentically? What makes you different from your best friend or sibling? Do you have a sense of yourself? Do you have inner confidence? Or are you disconnected from, or unclear about, who you really are? Are you clear on some of your interests, goals, or dreams?

Start where you are and look at yourself. Name what makes you unique, the things you care about or that interest you, because that is where your happiness lies. Your ✺*Workbook* is a place to explore those questions and answers.

No matter what your self-esteem is like today, know that your true self is your superpower, your secret weapon. You have a combination of interests, talents, and strengths that are completely unique to you. That combination will allow you to do things other people don't. We'll go through these in depth in your ✺*Workbook*, but for now, if you write down one thing you are interested in, one talent you have, and one of your strengths—or three things you care about—you will catch a glimpse of the unique person you really are.

If you've become too busy for these, ignored them, or compared them to someone else's interests or abilities and found fault with yourself, then you have let go of some of your personal strength and are missing out on some of your own happiness. Going forward from here, you can change that. You can reclaim you!

This is about getting you back to the real you, about your empowerment. If you uncover, accept, and develop your unique interests, if you honor your authentic self at your age now, you are setting up what will happen in your future—happiness and well-being. When you are solid in yourself, you will weather your problems in a healthy way, far from living in the storms of reactive discontent.

Sometimes we view our differences as weird or odd when we compare them to people who don't have them or who hide them. Don't judge your differences; just acknowledge them. Remember that they are actually your superpowers and your tools. Consider page 3 in the ✺*Workbook* your *home base*. Add to it when you can! And next time things aren't going your way or you are feeling low, read it over until you feel a bit better and take a step or two toward making those things part of your day. When you are doing that, take the time to enjoy it. Allow those things to shift or ignite your mood!

When You Are Not in Charge

Maybe change seems difficult to imagine. Maybe right now you are not in control of your schedule and circumstances. However, you still are, and will be, in charge of your reactions and of finding and growing your own happiness.

When you are in your parents' home, they run the house; in school, it's the teachers and administrators; at work, it's your boss. But what is your role? What is your responsibility in what isn't going the way you want it to? Have you come up with a great solution to an obvious problem? Have you spoken up about what isn't working for you to someone who can help? How do *you* react to your family? What are you contributing? How much are you getting from your classes or job? Do you like your boss or instructor? Will you be a good boss or teacher yourself one day? This isn't about self-blame or finding fault. It is about self-awareness, personal responsibility, and choosing your response instead of simply reacting.

A great deal is in your control now, which means that you can be kind, centered, and clear about your position in the face of imperfection, and if things don't feel right to you, you can start looking for where you will go next that is a better fit for you.

If you want an interesting and rewarding job, imagine what that might be for you. What would you love to do and get paid for? If you are in high school, start honestly looking ahead for the great trade school, enterprise, college, or service that sounds great to you and will be a correct social, intellectual, and creative fit for you. Find your tribe. Find out what those places require for admission and take the necessary steps to accomplish that before you apply. Have fun taking those interesting steps toward what you want to achieve! The process is your life! If you are in college, look at every major your college offers and imagine yourself a specialist in each field. How does each feel? Or start thinking about where you would love to live when you graduate. Imagine your options and a few unusual choices. What *feels* good or exciting?

If your parents want you to become a dentist, and they are paying for your education, and you want to be an orchestra conductor, consider majoring in one and minoring in the other. Maybe plan to make the choice for yourself in your junior year, or plan a double major! Be thankful your parents are supporting you, and be honest with yourself regarding how you feel about their goals for you. If you are interested in training, working, or living abroad, then take the time to find out what programs include that and what you need to do to qualify. The point is that you are in control of identifying where you want to go and taking steps to get there. Your plans and your intentions matter. Sometimes there is a price to pay for going your own way financially or in family dynamics. Weigh your priorities. What you are thinking, doing, and participating in now is setting up what will happen next. If you don't know what you want, just continue moving forward toward what matters to you and interests you—what you care about—and your life will unfold.

A Quick Glance at College

Not everyone will go to college. Some people need to go straight to work, some people stay home and care for family, others don't see the point in it, and still others jump right into activities that don't require an education or degree. There are many avenues for success, learning, and self-discovery, which we'll discuss throughout the book. Right now I'd like to share some ideas about college as a place to discover and strengthen interests and abilities.

If you don't know what you would love to do as a career or life interest, college can be an amazing place to discover that. Even if you already know what you want to do for paid work and it doesn't require a college degree, going to college or university can still be worthwhile to broaden your knowledge so that you can be better at what you want to do. College isn't job training; college is about diverse subjects and information. It's about learning things you don't know now—some things you've never imagined! College is about becoming an informed, well-rounded person. Right now, you don't know what you don't know. You don't know what you might learn, things that will inspire you that you haven't even heard of, or who you might meet who could send your life in a wonderful direction. College shouldn't be regarded as drudgery or an obligation; it is worldly exposure, and it can be an important part of discovering paths or paid careers doing something you would love to do.

Once you start working for a living, you will do that for most of your life, so why not decide on a city or country where you would love to live and consider colleges and universities there, to broaden yourself and strengthen your access to your interesting and meaningful life?

You Are Truly Unique

Your life is all about you. You are like a fingerprint, different from everybody else in the most remarkable and simple ways. And like every other person in the world, whether you know it or not, you have an inner calling to explore and actualize your unique talents and interests—an inner calling made up of what you care about and what interests you. And the world deserves what you have to offer. So today, beginning now, start making friends with your unique self and explore what interests you, because you will be making a difference in the world.

Put your best foot forward. Health, vitality, a friendly attitude, expressive clothes, and grooming are all elements of attractiveness that come from making an effort. If you look in the mirror and there are things you feel don't represent the real you, then you get to express yourself or accessorize your appearance the way that feels right to you. You get to present yourself the way you imagine feels best.

This is not about changing into someone else, or spending way too much money on the latest sneakers, or going away to a fitness program for three weeks. This is about owning and developing the authentic you. If you like beautiful colors, wear them. If a business suit looks cool to you, grab one from a thrift store and try it out for a day. If you have straw-straight or curly hair, own that and get a good haircut. If you are shorter or taller than you feel comfortable with, accept that it is what it is and figure out how to rock it. There isn't a person alive who is perfect or has every quality or characteristic they could want. But you'll see some people who present what they've got well and others who slouch and cover up, hide, or ignore what they've got. Which of those would you choose for yourself? Who would you hire? If you want to dye your hair for fun or get a haircut *you* think is cool, do it if it doesn't actively conflict with the job or school you are in. In that case, after work or school, do your thing! Take the steps to make yourself the best you can be with what you've got and where you are. Accept yourself, improve what you can, and always choose what makes *you* feel good—even if it's just a small step.

Money Can't Buy Happiness

A happy, authentic, and fulfilled life is not limited to or defined by financial success or owning expensive things. Period.

There are people who act cool by appearing rich, wearing the latest fashions, and driving an expensive car—and chances are they are covering insecurities and pain just like everyone else and may easily end up with financial debt that you don't want. Having enough money to meet your needs does eliminate the stresses of material need, so it's certainly a worthy goal, but if you pursue your personal interests and excellence in what matters to you, financial compensation will come organically and proportionately if you pursue it as a career. Just as being famous is a product of some form of achievement and not a sustainable job by itself, earned wealth comes from the exchange of money for goods or services, not an end goal without a means. Having enough money for your needs is important. Thinking that getting rich and having money will make you happier just isn't accurate. So consider not making your goals about money and instead making your goals about personal fulfillment and excellence in your interests. Then make good financial choices (more on that in chapter 5), and the rest will follow.

Heads-up. It is really easy to waste money doing and buying unnecessary things, as if spending time shopping and paying for amusement is just *normal life*.

In fact, your time and energy are far better spent on what matters to you, with those material things being reserved as special treats. If you eat out every night, it's not special, so saving it, or anything, for a special time becomes a financial and personal win. If you need to save more of your income, take a look at your habits. Everyone deserves to treat themselves periodically, but meanwhile, learn to cook well at home, automatically pay into a personal savings account every time you get any money, shop as a necessity or treat and not a social activity, teach yourself what you don't know (like how to change the oil in your car!), turn lights off that you aren't using, put on a sweater instead of extra heat in the whole house, shop at thrift stores instead of department stores, and appreciate commercial items without owning them. There are many simple tricks to keeping your money, which will help you get ahead!

What Are You Attracting or Broadcasting?

What message do you send to people who look at you? Are you authentic or hiding? Let's say you are interested in somebody you think is remarkable, but they are not interested in you. In some way, you are not in sync with them, you don't make sense to them, or their interests are elsewhere. If you want someone to notice you, become your best self, and if they notice you then, great. If not, so be it. Instead of silently longing for something or someone you don't have, step outside yourself, be as objective as you can, and ask yourself, "Is this about me, or is it about them?" Maybe it's just not the right moment; maybe the other person is going through something you can't see. Not everything is personal. By all means, present the way you'd love to be seen and smile genuinely at the people who interest you.

You might choose to improve yourself in areas that authentically appeal to the people who interest you (let's say you could become more athletic, or funny, or share their interests). Or you might want to honor who you authentically are and look at why you are interested in certain people in the first place. Maybe you actually have little in common and wouldn't be happy, or maybe they just have something you wish you had.

Don't settle for wishing! Either take steps to obtain what you want or accept that it's not in your life and celebrate *what is* with those who enjoy who you really are!

You are fun and interesting. You simply need to find the people who share your interests! Today is the day to look at yourself—face yourself. If you have been downplaying yourself in any way, then it is time to accept and rock your unique self. Be fun in the way you think is fun. Do what you think is interesting. See who shows up. Believe me, you are already remarkable and wonderful; it's just a matter of owning and developing it.

When you develop yourself, when you claim your unique gifts, talents, interests, and abilities, when you are actualized, then compatible people are attracted to you because you are in sync with them. That's a great truth about life. When you are downplayed, you are not being true to yourself, and you are out of sync with your unique self. Which would you choose? See yourself clearly as you are and also as you want to be. Hold that healthy, authentic vision and take the first steps toward it from where you are. Act now as if you already are as remarkable as you are going to grow to be.

Act As If

Acting as if you already are who you want to be is an amazing tool for starting on the path to where you want to go. This is not pretending to be someone you aren't. This is owning who you plan to become. Next time you go for a job interview, or to present your work, or to ask for support, imagine how it would be if you already had the job, the good grade, the promotion, the loan, the thing you want, and go to the meeting dressed and with the feeling of already being successful in that area. Present strongly, as if you already are what you want to be. Let's say you love animals, cooking, or art supplies, and you are applying for a related job where they will need to train you and you'll learn more. Imagine and feel what it would be like to be a professional in the field, and then go in acting with confidence in your interests and your ability to learn and contribute positively to their business or organization.

I remember my early jobs as a film set still photographer. I had to interview and show up with confidence I didn't have. I wasn't conning them. I knew I was going to succeed, but I also knew that if I went in showing my insecurities and inexperience, I wouldn't get the chance to rise to the occasion! So I figured out what I, as a photographer, would dress like, practical and with a creative aesthetic, in clothes that weren't brand-new and right off the rack but had the appearance like I'd worn them at work before. I visited film sets and saw how people dressed for work, and I matched what I liked, adding subtle, creative flare like good color, design, or a piece of interesting jewelry that showed my personal taste. I braced myself and walked in with an air of calm confidence, even though inside I was super nervous! I knew nervousness and shyness wouldn't contribute to the situation, but calmness and my abilities would; so I acted as if I had done it a hundred times, and I gave it my best.

The Complexities of Personal Problems

Some of you reading this have experienced real difficulties and trauma. I'm truly sorry. You did not deserve it, and you were not responsible for it happening. The good news is that there are ways to heal and grow, leaving that behind rather than enduring or suppressing it. There are resources for help and healing available to you, some of which I've listed in appendix 1, and I strongly encourage you to explore your community for professionals and groups whose inspired purpose is to support health and well-being. In chapter 6, "Cleaning Up Messes," I've outlined simple ways that you can start to work on your emotional and psychological health and coming to terms with your past. I have met amazing people who have done solid personal work and are now strong, centered, and wiser—better, not bitter.

There are thousands of stories of successful people who overcame serious adversities and now flourish. My teachers Jack Canfield, Annaliese Reid, and Deborah King are great examples, each with remarkable personal stories of moving from serious challenges to personal success, including overcoming abuse, a terminal diagnosis, and starting with only a goal and debt. I've added their information in appendix 2 if you want specific examples. I look forward to sharing a few ways to clear your heart and mind and move toward what you will love to be true. Starting wherever you are at now, intend to heal past problems and triggered reactions so that you can enjoy a life that feels good to you.

Intend, not wish, because there is real power in being purposeful.

If It's Happening, You Can Handle It

Every situation or event is an opportunity for you to recognize where you stand and to act from that position. There is an expression—*life is happening for you, not to you.* And another, *you are an energetic match for what you are calling in,* meaning if it's happening, even if it's difficult, you can handle it and grow from it. These are philosophical concepts but worth considering. What's the takeaway from a bad situation?

What's the nugget of truth you can discover? What can you do to create change for the better?

Life brought you to today. Life happened, and it led you to this point of knowing you want to build a great life in a custom way.

Your life is unique, and you know things that other people don't know. There are things that matter to you that don't matter to other people. You have had hardships, and you have had successes and special experiences and relationships. All that is what led you to where you are today. And now you get to start choosing the things that have meaning to you and that make you feel good. You get to choose happiness and create—deliberately build—a life for yourself that is filled with things that make sense to you, things that you want for yourself and for a better world. There will be some difficulties along the way, because life is dimensional and instructional, and there are many factors at play, but you are gaining awareness, and you will have the tools to take life's twists in stride and still wake up feeling good most mornings. Congratulations!

Finding Faults Doesn't Serve You

Another key principle you can start with today is, from this day on, do not compare yourself to anyone else and then judge or diminish yourself. Period. No good comes of it, and it is disempowering. Whatever age you are, you may just be an undeveloped version of yourself.

You are not better than anyone, and you are certainly not less than anyone. If there is something you like, it's because it makes sense to you, you resonate with it; try out whatever it is, and if it fits, keep it. It is important to notice what you like, what feels right to you, and to give yourself permission to be it or enjoy it. There is so much bad feeling involved in comparing and despairing, and bad feelings are not an accurate gauge of value! If you fully develop and actualize your authentic self, and someone else does too, you are going to be different! So appreciate or admire that different person and leave it there.

You might see someone whose clothes you like more than your own, or who knows what they want to be when they are older, and you might compare yourself with them and feel less than, as I did. You may be different regarding some things that you like, but believe me, you are *not* less than. You are simply different and possibly still developing and evolving. From this moment on, drop judgmental comparison and stay with appreciation of differences. And if you catch yourself comparing yourself to someone else, notice it, figure out what you like about them, and leave it there. If you think you might like to change something about yourself for the better, that's your prerogative. Go for it. But toss out comparative fault finding, starting right now.

Going Forward

Intend to explore and understand these three things about yourself: What do you *care* about? What makes you *feel* good? And how might you be holding yourself back now?

Most people pay no attention to those concepts and spend every day simply reacting to what happens around them, whether they like it or not. When people live like that, life doesn't bring happiness on a platter. Yet when you decide what you want and choose your idea of happiness, you will experience positive outcomes.

Make peace with the past, work and live in the present, and create a happy future. Today is exactly the right day to begin making changes toward being your authentic self and having the life you want. Declare to yourself, and in your ✍*Workbook* on page 4, what you are not happy with, what you would love to be different, and how you would love it to be!

Going forward from today, if you had a magic wand and could change things in your life, what would they be? In the next chapter, we'll look at specifically what you'd love to change, eliminate, or add to your life in order for it to feel great to *you!*

Somewhere on the inside cover of your ✍Workbook, in the right size and color, draw an image that signifies you are starting! Or write "Starting Where I Am" or "SWIA!" Include today's watershed date. You are on your way!

❧*W*❧

In the ❧*Workbook*, on page 4, you'll write down what you think would be personal improvements. These are things you would change about yourself, like eating more healthily, being more patient, or keeping your head up and eyes forward. Only kindness here! What would make you your best self? And after those are written out, you'll write some ideas or steps it will take to make the changes.

In the ❧*Workbook*, on page 5, write down the things that you like about yourself. Even add some true improvements that you have started making or plan to make, as if they are already coming true; the seeds have been planted on those, so own them. Imagine any self-doubts, insecurities, or fears released. Describe yourself as you visualize your fully wonderful, deep-down real, authentic self. What are your strengths and good traits? What do you like about yourself? These can be big and obvious or small lights glimmering in your heart or mind.

In the ❧*Workbook*, on page 6, list three or more important things that you would *change* in your life right now if you could. What is missing in your life? What is happening that you don't enjoy and you'd get rid of? What isn't going the way you want it? What went wrong that you would like to fix or improve? Think about changing for the better!

In the ❧*Workbook*, on page 6, in the second column, write some of the good aspects of what you wrote in the first column. Almost everything has pros and cons, good and bad aspects. It's important to look at things as a whole, not just at the good or bad.

Chapter Three

If You Had a Magic Wand

Because as much as Brave Thinkers are focused
on their dream, they also hold on to the promise
of "This or something better still."

—Mary Morrissey, from her Brave Thinking Institute blog
https://www.bravethinkinginstitute.com/blog

L et's look honestly at what bothers you about your current
life and the path you see yourself on, as well as what you *like*
about now and what you would love to have in your future.

Imagine You Have a Magic Wand

You will be exploring this further in the ☙*Workbook* soon, but for
now, just imagine you have a magic wand that you can use to change
or fix anything in your life right now. What would you wave it at?
What things do you feel that if you fixed, changed, or eliminated,
then you would be happier now?

And if you could wave your wand and create a future that seems
wonderful to you, what would it include? Where would you live?
Who would you keep in your life? Who would you see less often

or not at all? What is your job? What are you doing to make things better for the community or planet, or for a group or issue you think is important? What matters to you so much that no matter what else is going on, you feel this one thing must be part of your life going forward? Imagine the most fun part of your future life. Will you surf, or go dancing with friends, or ride a bicycle or horse in gorgeous places, or read in a hammock with a cat sleeping at your side? What would you love to do—and where?

At one point, my new, better life was having a meaningful job I could look forward to each day, where I made enough money never to worry about needs, and I would actually make enough more for travel. I wanted the right possessions (few, useful, and beautiful). I wanted better relationships at home. I wanted a healthy, yoga-limber body and free time to explore and have adventures. I wanted to connect to my intuition and centered clarity regarding what matters to me. I wanted to be happy.

Perhaps your vision is not completely clear yet. What if you don't know what you want or what you are good at and care about? What if you sense that something is missing from your life, but you don't know what it is? Perhaps you have fears. Do you feel something is lacking? What went wrong that you would like to be better? What would you wave that wand at? How do you feel in your life now, what really matters to you?

The Power of Asking Questions

We need to ask questions if we want to receive answers and clarity. If you don't ask, if you just coast along or do nothing, if your thoughts and actions are random, what comes up in your life will be random. But if there is something specific you want to know, then the first step is to actually ask yourself, a mentor, parent, teacher, or friend about it. Whether you are feeling private about it or not, as a first step, ask it like a question to your true self, or to the great unknown, like a prayer to your deepest self. Hold still and really wonder about it, imagine it, and ask in your mind or out loud.

A Quick Look at What's Bothering You

In the ✎*Workbook*, on page 6, you started a list of what you *don't* like about what is happening in your life today. It is important to acknowledge what you don't like, and it is important not to dwell on it. What do you call "my problems"? Listing what you don't like in your life is a great way to clarify what you need to fix or distance yourself from in order to feel better. Add to page 6 in the ✎*Workbook* each time you realize something isn't working for you—anything you would wave your wand at if you could.

Not long from now, you will have less time to participate in those negative things because you will have set them right, and you'll be busy with other things you love to do!

The Pros and Cons of Now

Think for a minute if there are good aspects of the things you don't like. Almost everything has both pros and cons, good and bad aspects. It's important to look at things as a whole, not only at one side of something. "My mother is driving me crazy" seems definitive and without option, but it almost always has a flipside like "so I'm spending more time with my father" or "but she's trying her best, and I just need to figure out why I'm so annoyed." By purposefully identifying good components or results in things that are bothering you, you'll gain objectivity, seeing the big picture instead of being trapped in the negative details. Doing this can give you more patience or help clarify what is bothering you so that you can address it. Greater understanding helps shift the problem and can actually take some of the negative charge off of the bad side—not so that you can endure it better, but so that you can step out of reactive behavior and into making your own constructive choices.

Sustained Thoughts and Emotions Create Results

If, day in and day out, you are tolerating something that bothers you, you are spending too much time feeling bad about it, and it is unhealthy on several levels. Sustained thoughts or emotions, good or bad, tell our brains and minds that this subject is important, and we begin to notice or attract other things that are "important" in the same way. It's as literal as if you are sad about something in the news, and you tell people about it, making them sad, they will begin to tell you more sad things because you are all experiencing this sadness as important. You are all sad until the subject changes. Instead, if you notice something that makes you uncomfortable, acknowledge it, accept that it is what it is, and then move on toward a solution or change the subject to something constructive. If you do that, you will spend less time every day tolerating that something uncomfortable. That is where you are headed.

I'm asking you to start to be aware of where your thoughts dwell, and if that is not a happy place, interrupt the negative thoughts and feelings by changing your thoughts to an upside of the situation, to what you *do* want, to what you are working toward and looking forward to. When you catch yourself dwelling on what is bothering you, purposefully shift your thoughts to acknowledging that you were just thinking about them and then move on; do not settle for simply dwelling on things you feel bad about.

Imagine It the Way You Want It

There is a difference between intellectually deciding to do something and following an established path to achieve it and visualizing something the way you'd love it, getting excited, and doing what it takes to make it happen.

That is something many people don't know, and it is something that many successful people purposefully use as a tool for advancement.

What if things had already changed to the way you want them? How would that feel? Imagine clearly that each of your uncomfortable areas are completely fixed—things are the way you want them—and *feel* how nice it is that each thing is now the way you would love it to be. Imagine it clearly and enjoy all the details. For example, "I am so happy I took the time to clean my room! It looks great, and it's so much more comfortable!" Or "I am so happy I found a good therapist! It feels great to get stuff off my chest, and I actually have less stress when I'm going out with friends now."

Take a moment to imagine and enjoy a personal goal right now. See every detail!

In doing that, you are actually actively taking a step toward change. It is part of how our minds work and part of how life works! It's like imagining a trip to an exciting place you would love to go! See yourself there and enjoy the way it looks, the food, the music, the breeze. For some people, doing that instinctively leads to action—to buying tickets or saving up money. They don't settle for wishing; they get excited and are inspired to take steps to make it happen. What we can really imagine and get excited about has wings. *It works for every aspect of your life where you clearly and repeatedly imagine things the way you want them and start heading in that direction with the first indicated steps.* It may take a week, a month, or a year, depending on what it is and how many other people are involved, but if you do this every day, progress must and will come.

Understand that you may not get exactly what you want exactly when you want it. It depends on how big the idea or change is. But if you take steps, you always get somewhere beyond where you are today. The clearer the thing you've imagined, the more direct the steps are and the faster the change comes. Sometimes you get somewhere better than your wildest dreams of today—like I did with my surprise career of film set photography and later as an energy release practitioner!

Starting today, when you think of something good that you really want, imagine and feel it is already real; feel the good feelings that go along with it.

For fun, try picking a small, obtainable thing that you want to do or want to change. Imagine it, write it down, and write what you need to do to get it. Then do what you wrote down. Like "I want to put nice plants in that patch of bare earth." Then "Buy drought-resistant plants, gardening claw and trowel, small bag of organic soil conditioner, and a watering can. Block off Saturday morning, and call Lauren to come do it with me." Or, "I want to stop my negative self-talk." Then "When I catch myself doing it, I notice it, and I say to myself, 'Ha-ha, I just did it again,' and then I immediately get back to whatever it is that I was actually doing at the time." You can use page 8 in the *Workbook* for this, now or at the end of the chapter.

You will see how the small thing you wanted to do or change will shift and then change into what you took action toward. Even if it takes time. This process works for all positive changes. Some things take longer to change than others, and sometimes the change comes in a form you can't even imagine now. Sometimes things can be difficult before they get better. No matter how the shift happens, if you are holding positive intentions, it will shift toward those.

Why is this important? This is about anything in your life you want to change or create. Imagine your perfect job, or how you want to be living three years from now, or improving your current living conditions for next year. If you can imagine it, if you can get excited about it, if you can start making some plans, you will bring it or something parallel into being.

This is not to say that you will get everything you want. If your goal is that your neighbors' house turns upside down, it's not going to happen. This is about visualizing creative, satisfying, and positive change. You may want to become an acclaimed musician, and you may become one, or you may end up as part of a rocking local group or making a living teaching music at the most progressive music institute there is. You don't know what doors will open to you, which doors you will want to walk through, or where you will end up; but know that if you have determination, intention, and joy about something you want, interesting things in that realm will come your way, maybe something even better than you can imagine right now!

If You Don't Know What You Want

It's okay if you don't yet know what you want in some area of your life. What if you're not sure what you want to do for a living when you're older? What if you don't know what you are good at or what matters to you? What if you don't know where you want to train, or what you would want to study, or what type of person would fit well as a partner? Pick the area you are uncertain about and let yourself dream and visualize. If you have trouble imagining what you want, start by asking yourself, "Is what I have now the way I want it to be five years from now? What would I want to be different? What would I eliminate? What would I add?" Visualize your life with those changes. There is power in imagining things the way you would like them to be, especially if you jot down notes about it, draw it, write a poem, make a list, then visualize it often, visit where you'd like it to take place, and imagine yourself there with friends. Little by little, this type of visualization helps you learn what you'd love to be true.

Your ✎Workbook Is Your Magic Wand

You do have a magic wand; it's your intention. That's what changes things from the way they are now to the way you want them to be. And for now, your wand is your ✎Workbook, where it will all be written out by you, for you. Good ideas that show up with inspiration and conviction in your ✎Workbook now will show up in your fulfilling life later because you have brought them into existence yourself.

Do you know what matters most to you? Is it friendship or freedom, a healthy planet or dancing? Do you know what you really care about? Is it wild animals or strays, marine biology or windsurfing—or all of those? Are there issues in the news that you think are really important, while others you skim past? Did you know that if you combine your personal interests and talents with what matters to you, you create a compound of excellence, a force of nature? In the next chapter, we'll have a look at that and customize it to you!

On the inside cover of your ✎Workbook, somewhere, in the right size and color, draw your magic wand and write today's magic date.

❧ *W* ☙

❧ *Workbook Exercises for Chapter 3*

In the ❧ *Workbook*, on page 7, for each of the things you listed on page 6, write a statement in the present, as if it is already the way you want it. For example, "I am so happy that I took all my old stuff to the thrift store, and now I've got so much more space!" Imagine clearly that each of your uncomfortable areas are resolved and what you'd rather have is in place, and *feel* how nice it is that each thing is now the way you would love it to be.

In the ❧ *Workbook*, on page 8, write down one small, doable thing that you want to do or change in your life and what the steps are to make it happen.

In the ❧ *Workbook*, on page 9, write out four things, big or small, that you would love to fill your future with, or to fill your life with now, and some steps you can take toward achieving that. Reread and feel the statement on page 9, number 2, at least once every day, until it has come true or its equivalent has happened and you don't need to keep working toward it anymore. Take steps toward it daily, small or large.

In the ❧ *Workbook*, on page 10, you'll find specific questions about what you are unsure and sure of and the space to write out solutions, big or small, as if they are already true. This is not the moment to think about *how* you could accomplish all your dreams, hopes, and intentions; this is the time to start really looking at what makes you feel great when you think of it.

Chapter Four

What Really Matters?

Unused talents are corrosive.

—Frances Merewether Power Weismiller, my
mother, who attributed it to Carl Jung

I was a sophomore at a good college, streamlining for pre-med, when I found chemistry so difficult that it was killing my GPA and stressing me greatly, and I also started feeling like something else wasn't right about that major for me. I should have gotten a chemistry tutor! But that aside, increasingly, something that I couldn't put my finger on wasn't feeling right. I knew I wanted to help people, and my grandfather had been a surgeon, so on the one hand, it seemed like a worthy and attainable goal. Yet the thought of the sterile offices and hospitals, the quality of the fluorescent light, the anonymous pastel scrub uniforms, the anguishing patients and grueling hours—these imaginings were dampening my dream. When I visualized my future, I didn't like what I was seeing. So, as I described in chapter 1, I decided to take one semester at a junior year abroad program in France to study art, cuisine, and poetry! I knew that by the end of that, I would either know I didn't want to be a medical doctor or I would have adequately broadened myself to make me an even better physician!

It was the best semester of my education, one of the great times of my life. I loved the artistic pursuits, the fellow students, the food, the culture, and the challenge of a second language. I felt like I was where I belonged, and I wished it had been the whole year! And when it was over, I knew that I had wanted to be a doctor for the wrong reasons. I had wanted to do it because it was respected and helpful, not because it was my calling or passion. Panicking for a new major, serendipitously there was a new major just created called audiovisual communications that my creative electives from France applied to, so I jumped on it. It wasn't a passion either; it was an interesting port in a storm, but the courses sounded fun and creative, and I'd end up graduating with a marketable skill (which was a relief, because at that point I really didn't have one). Getting my BA in audiovisual communications led me to apply to and get accepted to one of the best film schools in the country—USC Film School, where George Lucas went and which Steven Spielberg endowed. Those are contemporary filmmakers I respected, and their involvement seemed like an endorsement of quality education and training to me. I ended up with a master's of fine arts degree in film production and loved filmmaking!

It was a circuitous route, but I followed my heart and my instincts about what was right for me. Even if it wasn't one intention or one goal, each step of the way, I had intentions and I met the goals I made, or I wasn't afraid to make new ones. It illustrates my earlier point; in the beginning, you may not even imagine the amazing place you will end up, but if you set goals honoring your unique self and take indicated steps, you are sure to end up somewhere true to you personally—and not with just a dream on a couch!

When you are trying to change your life or build a life you will love to live, it's important to take the time to figure out what really matters to you and which people, places, and things seem right for you. Because can you really be happy without those? Some people adore animals, some people need to be able to jump on a bike and ride long distances, some people want to walk to cafés and small, local grocery stores, and some people thrive in the operating room! We are all different. The things that make us happy are different, and it is important to know what yours are.

This Matters

What are some important things that you care about, that really matter to you, or you think are cool? What made you happy recently?

The things that make you happy and seem exciting are clues to building a life you'll enjoy. The things you care about and that interest and matter to you are guides to what you want in your fulfilling life. Maybe one area will be your dream job, and the other will be where you have fun with friends. And if something matters to you, interests you, *and* makes you happy—it's magic! This is all about what resonates for you.

If you could solve any problem that you are aware of in the world, what might you want to fix or be remembered for resolving? What if you were the person to solve the problem of nutritionally depleted agricultural soil because you care about future generations' health and you love being out in nature? Notice every time something you care about or enjoy shows up for you. Keep noticing what you notice and add them to page 2 (The Happy List) and/or 12 (This Matters! list) of your 🐾*Workbook*!

Feeling Grateful Matters

Here is something that matters for well-being: taking time to appreciate what is currently good in your life. Take a minute and search your thoughts and feelings. In what areas are you fortunate enough to actually feel grateful? Some people are grateful for love, some for smiles, others for home cooking, and others for a chance to help people who need it. Believe it or not, the experience of feeling grateful has an impact. If you can generate the feeling of gratitude and attach it to the things that are important to you, you are telling your subconscious and conscious mind, "This is important," and that you want to notice it, find it, and have it.

Next time you have to make a choice between two or more things, you can ask yourself, "How do I feel about each of these choices? Which one(s) would I be most grateful to have in my life or have knowledge about?" The answer to that question is a good deciding factor. And if there is one you would not be grateful for, it's an easy one to rule out!

When we choose what affects us positively, the things we are grateful for, what we care about, and what we enjoy, we lay the groundwork for their part in our future.

Providence Is Moving

Let me take a minute to define three concepts we will be looking at: providence, coincidence, and synchronicity. Some people believe they have significance greater than the obvious, and others believe they are straightforward. Either way, they have bearing and impact.

With a lower case, *providence* can be defined as purposeful preparation for future eventualities. Future eventualities—that is what we are purposefully creating. When capitalized, *Providence* is defined as nature, God, or universal law and as providing protective assistance. The idea is that there is a protective, constructive force in life that plays out unseen.

Coincidence can be defined as a concurrence of events or circumstances without connection.

Synchronicity can be defined as the simultaneous occurrence of events that appear significantly related yet have no observable connection.

Many people dismiss unseeable causal connections as mere unrelated flukes. But that is no more accurate than disbelieving in radio waves because you can't see them. Providence, coincidence, and synchronicity are part of life. They are circumstances you experience.

This quote by Scottish mountaineer and writer William Hutchison Murray (1913–1996) expresses ideas I love:

> The moment one definitely commits oneself, then Providence moves too. All sorts of things occur to help one that would never otherwise have occurred. A whole stream of events issues from the decision, raising in one's favor all manner of unforeseen incidents and meetings and material assistance, which no man could have dreamt would have come his way.

Straightforward or not, how wonderful that life works this way. I've experienced it!

As you begin to focus your attention on yourself, your interests, and your unique path, begin also to write down anything that seems like coincidence or synchronicity on page 13 in the ✍*Workbook*. At first, you may not notice any, but if you open your attention to this and start writing them down, you will begin noticing unexpected and unusual concurrences. They are part of the shift over to your correct path. They are providence at work, and it is interesting and helpful to be aware and watch this unfold. Next time someone says, "The weirdest thing just happened," perk up your ears. You will start to notice that synchronicities and alignments are part of life, unseen but experiential, and how you can tell you are on the right path. Synchronicity is the *how* in action. "I am going to Italy next year. I don't know how, but I'm going to get there!" The longer you notice and make note of synchronicities and coincidences, the more you will see that there is an uncanny connection between what matters to you, what you feel great about and intend, and doors opening for those things to occur.

Make It Happen!

Here is one more definition for you. The word *manifest* can be defined as to occur, materialize, be revealed, or create. It involves going from an idea to a tangible actuality. There are people who get things done, who make things happen, who are productive. They are called manifesters. For example, born in 1856, inventor Nikola Tesla was an electrical and mechanical engineer and a futurist known for his part in the invention of household electricity, specifically the everyday alternating current (AC) electricity supply system that runs American homes and cities. He lived when light came from oil-burning lanterns and there was no electricity in buildings or on streets. Each of his inventions, like all inventions, started as an idea. Then he figured out how to make it possible, and then he created it, bringing it into the tangible world. Tesla manifested electricity in the home. You are a manifester as well. From the tangible to the abstract, you are manifesting all the time, and now you have begun manifesting a life you will love living. In your 🖋*Workbook*, you are collecting lists of ideas based on what really matters to you so that you can manifest them specifically!

Your Unique Talents

Now, consider what your talents are. I never knew what mine were, and nobody ever asked me or told me. But of course I had talents, and in time, they emerged. I am a successful photographer because I persist in mastering technology and I see moments in time. My best photographs are when I catch expressive emotions and gestures I see in the split second before they change. As I was growing up, I certainly never knew I had that talent; it certainly wasn't anything anybody talked to me about or that I set out to achieve. Maybe we could say my talent is empathy, and my strength is perseverance.

I am asking you to start noticing your talents now. Are you well organized? Do you have a feeling for colors and shapes? Do your friends turn to you when they have a problem? Are you good at thinking up fun things for the weekend? Do you like strategy games? Do you love to dance or laugh? Were you good at the piano when you were a kid?

What are you good at? Jot down your answers now or later on page 14 in the 🖋*Workbook*.

And to turbocharge that idea, how can that strength or talent be used to help? For example, if you have a good ear for music, you could become a DJ and play happy dance music so people can blow off stress and feel good dancing, or an orchestra conductor so people have access to excellent or innovative live music. Your talent would be a gift to others! If you are good in the kitchen, you could start a cool destination diner or become a chef in personal homes, on yachts or freighter ships, or at retreats so people can eat well and therefore think well.

If you have a talent or ability that you are not developing and using, you are missing an important level of opportunity for success and satisfaction. It's too good to miss out on. Maybe you haven't found how it serves you yet. Let's discover that! My mother hung a card in a common area of our home that read "Unused talents are corrosive – Carl Jung" meaning perhaps that they ache and bother unless and until you acknowledge them, and if unused, you are unfulfilled, which has bad feelings built in. Your talents and strengths, the things you are good at, are hints and clues for your happy path in life. You are or will be good at something special, because you are unique, and there are people out there who need your unique talents and abilities. By the way, my mother attributed that quote to Carl Jung, but I have searched high and low to see where he wrote that. Maybe she ingeniously thought we'd take it seriously only if it came from him, not her!

No matter how big or small your talent is, if you enjoy it, if it comes easily to you or you feel empowered striving for it, you have a gratifying future including it. Read that sentence again.

Envision and feel how you would if you could use your talents daily—maybe at home with your family, in your community, or on a large scale and while helping people or nature. Really imagine it, visualize it, and feel it. Good, right?

Your Unique Interests

The next step regarding what matters for you is to pay attention to what *interests* you. If you selected ten people at some very diverse fair or market, and you asked them to list their top five market booths of interest, you would see how different people are. Some people would be interested in the comic book booths, others in the artisan hat-making booth. What is important now is what *you* are interested in and attracted to in daily life, on the weekend, in movies, and in books.

Continue to notice what you notice in this context. You will notice a car full of people, a type of fruit, or a certain kind of dog you think is adorable. In that instant, there were thousands of things in your field of vision that you could have noticed, but you noticed what you noticed because somewhere in your heart or mind, it is meaningful for you. If it is a negative connection, if you saw it and it didn't feel good, acknowledge it, help the situation, or let it go. If it is a positive connection—for example, you like a car or the music or the type of people in it—ask yourself what you liked about it, what interested you.

Maybe some of these are just things you think are really cool whenever you hear about them—like hang gliding or growing organic produce for a local restaurant. List them if they are things you could actually enjoy doing. Imagine yourself enjoying doing these things, alone or with others, and sharing your successes with people who care about you. If you aren't sure, try it if you can, or keep it on the list, because you might!

> *Creative interests.* Creativity is usually associated with artistry and art, but it can be part of anything from cooking, music, or gardening to building an engine, putting together a team, or manifesting an idea.

> *Intellectual interests.* Intellectual just means anything pertaining to the mind, like learning, reasoning, understanding, and objective thinking. If you are interested in astronomy, the history of food, nature, the power of belief, how something works, mathematical

equations, the cities of the world—anything—you have an intellectual interest in it. This is about the joy of learning about things that interest you or that you care about.

Since you have creative and intellectual interests, large and small, it is extremely important to create time for them in your life! They make you feel happy, engaged, and fulfilled!

What are you interested in? What interests you that your friends can't do or that doesn't interest them? We are looking at all your true interests, not just the ones you share with others. Whether you feel great about your interests and abilities or not, they serve you. If you are good at math and some of your friends aren't, don't compare yourself. It's your talent! Embrace whatever talents or interests you have. How would it feel if you got paid to work using talents that came to you naturally, while being around people who share your interests and while helping others? Imagine that. Visualize it. Feel how good that would feel! For example, I know a woman who loves her job being an accountant at a publishing firm because she gets to do what she's naturally good at and in a context that really interests her! Of course, this is not only about career and money, but if you work, I want you to enjoy it, so I keep bringing it up.

In all areas of your life, honoring your unique interests will pay off in contentment.

Of Longing and Discontent

We are striving for long-term contentment, happiness, and fulfillment. So if you find yourself experiencing discontent or longing, let's use them as indicators of need for change.

Longing is wishing for something so much it almost aches. Discontent is unhappiness with something the way it is now. Have you been longing and wishing for what you want, rather than doing anything about it? Have you been dissatisfied and unhappy about something, yet you just go on living with it because you believe you have no choice? This goes back to your "What you would change if you could?" list on page 4 in the ⚿*Workbook*. Longing for something and discontentment with something are clues that you need to rework things in order to be happy in those areas.

Don't settle for living with longing and discontent. Right now, you are shifting, catching yourself, moving to productive thoughts and good feelings. Notice what you long for and turn the solution or antidote into a statement. Instead of thinking, *I really wish I had a group of best friends*, notice what that wishing feels like—a bit sad and unfulfilled—and right then, say to yourself instead, "I would love to have a group of best friends. I can't wait to meet them or put that together," and feel how that feels. It feels better! Positive statements are instructions to your mind, your deep self, and to Providence. They are solution oriented and carry a positive feeling with them. You are noticing what you feel, and you are shifting negative longing and discontent into solution-oriented ideas that feel great!

Believe me, we all have doubts and negative thoughts, but our power is in noticing them and changing what we tell ourselves! Your life is an open book, a ship on a fair sea! At first, it might take effort to move from your usual discontent to creating purposeful solutions, but it's a necessary and valuable step. Soon, you will do it easily and comfortably, and you will be spending less time feeling unhappy! You will be telling your deep self what is really important to *you*. Take the time to feel the feelings of gratitude about the idea of meeting those friends and then move on with your day. Start noticing other people who are not moving beyond discontent—people who always complain or give energy to what is wrong with a situation. Soon, you will realize how negative that is, and you will start to step away, to step forward into what makes you feel good!

What Is a Feeling Actually?

Do you know what joy is? The simple answer is that it feels like a kind of happiness. But what is it really? Joy is an emotion, a feeling; you physically feel it, and it feels different from *angry*, which also has a specific feeling to it. Do you know what those distinct feelings actually are? They are not thoughts from your mind. Scientifically, per physics and quantum physics, feelings/emotions are the electromagnetic energetic frequency of chemical hormones our glands produce. We feel them physically; we don't think them, so they are called feelings. Different glands and organs produce different hormones and frequencies that we interpret as different feelings. This is a key concept in working toward and obtaining happiness, because if we are prone to feeling certain negative feelings, we can unlearn them—no matter which experiences started them. If we are aware of our circumstances, not reactive, then our organs and glands don't react with hormone production and feelings.

You may have heard someone say that everything is energy. Let's take time now to look at what that really means and what it means for you and your happiness. In nature, energy and energetic frequencies are scientifically quantitative and measurable. Every different thing has a unique energetic frequency that differentiates it from its opposite and other nonrelated things. When you take the life force energy out of someone or something, it perishes. With healthy energetic substances and experiences, it thrives. You are no different from anything else in nature in that way.

Feelings are energetic frequencies too. Let's look at the good and the bad, what's useful and what doesn't serve us well.

Taking a Look at Bad Feelings

Negative emotions and reactions are very important for us. They are part of how we keep ourselves safe and moving away from things that don't feel right to us. We are designed to experience and process them and move beyond them. However, when emotions are overwhelming or too intense, we often block and suppress them. In that case, the negative emotion hasn't been processed and passed; instead, it is retained and may repeat or trigger unless it is addressed and resolved.

Dr. Bradley Nelson calls these "trapped emotions" and explains in his book *The Emotion Code,*

> Most people are amazed to find that their emotional baggage is more literal than they imagined. Trapped emotions actually consist of well-defined energies that have a shape and form.

Scientifically and universally, everything is energy. Everything is made of energy on the subatomic level and has a measurable energetic frequency. That includes our thoughts and emotions. Emotions can become blocked energetically—trapped—when they are ignored, repressed, or denied. That's another important thing that nobody told me! It's important to feel all our emotions and to let them pass through us like an ocean wave or like steam rising and disappearing.

When we shut them down because they seem too strong or they hurt, that's when they stay with us, only to rise again and again until we acknowledge them and do our personal work to process and release them.

You can feel how anger *feels* different from sorrow and joy; you are in fact feeling their individual energetic frequencies. If we repeatedly think a certain thought or feel a certain feeling, we are repeatedly generating that energetic frequency in our bodies. And we broadcast these emotions unless we are purposefully hiding them. People register and react to the energetic frequencies of emotions like anger and joy, just like an eardrum registers a sound wave. Understanding this is important in overcoming your emotional obstacles, healing and strengthening yourself, and achieving your goals—because blocked emotions and truths will repeatedly resurface, often as obstacles in your life, until you have processed and released them normally.

Positive emotions are generated and processed the same way. So, to get back to the emotion of joy, it is a unique, quantifiable energetic frequency generally connected to the release of dopamine from your endocrine system. Joy is a feeling and frequency, as different from the frequency of anger as the frequencies of gentle classical music are from the intense frequencies of loud jackhammering and drilling. Why is this important?

Feel the Positive Emotions

It's important to experience the emotions that make us feel good. They are part of mental, emotional, and physical well-being. Take a minute to think of something particularly great from your Happy List on page 2 of your ☙*Workbook* and feel joy about it for a moment. What if you got a call right now saying, "Congratulations! It's yours forever!" Think about that and feel the pleasure of joy about it. Feel happy! Every time you take the time to feel happy about a good thing, you are telling your conscious and subconscious minds that there is a connection between that thing and joy/happiness, and then that thing is noted as important by your subconscious mind. You will start to notice steps to achieve it and other people who have it and enjoy it. In most cases, this is all that is needed for that good thing to start to become part of your life synchronistically.

It's not enough to sit on your couch and imagine with feeling; you must take the clear steps from where you are in that direction. For example, if you want to be a pilot flying medicine to rural communities, you need to research what the requirements to become a pilot are and then do what it takes to get that license. You have to be out there trying for the doors to open.

And can you imagine the difference between becoming a pilot because your parents are pressuring you to pick a prestigious career, versus taking the time to feel joy at each step of becoming a pilot because you want to fly? This is your life; choose joy in the process, and you will end up with joy in the outcome!

What if you need money, and someone tells you about a job doing something you don't want to do? And you get the job. Do you just say thank you for the opportunity to make some money to pay your bills, even though day in, day out, you are unhappy at work? Or do you say thank you and then, in all your free time, work hard to find a job in a field you feel interested in or good about?

When I started out as a photographer, I was grateful for any job that paid and gave me experience, and I worked on some movies I would never go see! But at a certain point, I limited my job search and acceptances to films with subjects or artists I felt good about.

Soon, I loved job after job as I found the ones that fit my aesthetic and temperament.

In some cases, it is as hard to get a bad job as a good one, so intend to look for a job doing something of interest, or apprentice or train in your field of interest. Don't just settle for what is randomly dropped in your lap if it does not actively appeal to you. Don't settle for something you would not choose for yourself. You can accept something as it is—that is your choice—but don't automatically settle by being unaware of its actual impact and what your options really are.

Action causes response, change occurs, and doors open. Doing nothing, waiting and hesitating, produces nothing. Sometimes you just have to act! If you are unsure of a job, take it! You might like it, or it might drive you to find a better one!

I'm just asking you to become aware of your choices and to look for what you want instead of passively accepting the first thing you hear of. Take it if you need the money, and feel good about that, but keep looking until you find a good match for you personally!

Worry versus Brainstorming

For considering problems and making choices, let's look at the differences between worrying and brainstorming. They are both generated in our minds, in our thoughts, often in response to bad news or an unfortunate circumstance. Worry is generally fear based and is ineffective for problem-solving because the worrisome problems and negative possibilities replay involuntarily in your mind, making you feel worse and worse. People fall into it because they believe their mind is reviewing and that they are considering, while in fact they are mostly just cycling fears. On the other hand, brainstorming is an active, important problem-solving tool used by many professionals, and purposefully coming up with diverse solutions can be exciting!

Right now, for a moment, feel worried about something. Remember a night you couldn't sleep and your mind was relentlessly worrying about something in your life. Worrying doesn't feel good. Now, think about brainstorming all the positive solutions to the same problem. With brainstorming, you are active in your power, and you feel engaged.

Worrying is not constructive evaluation. It has a negative feeling or frequency attached to it that is unpleasant. It rarely leads to constructive resolution, and it almost always leads to stress. The frequency of worry can become memorized (or trapped) and will repeat itself whenever you come into contact with something that reminds you of that thing you were worrying about. If you catch yourself worrying, by all means notice it. Then create a shift with positive instructional thinking.

For example, if you have a test at school and you are worried, the worry might be your worst problem and cause you to do worse. Instead, you could say and feel, "I've got this, and an hour from now, I'll be through it!" And feel how great it is to feel good about it! Stay with the good feeling, and your mind will be clearer as you take the test. Or, let's say you never studied and don't think you can pass, well then, why worry? At that point, it is what it is. Give it your best shot. Come in strong and do your best. You never know! Either way, stop worrying and walk into the test intending to do the best you can! Feel the intention.

If you have time, *brainstorm* your success. What are three things you can do to be closer to success? You can get a good night's sleep, review the end-of-chapter notes, and take five minutes to clear your mind and relax before entering the test room.

Journaling is a great way to move beyond worry! Write your worries down. Thoroughly describe them and hash through all the details. Write how they make you feel and why. You'll feel better just getting them out! Journaling often helps to *process* your concerns so that you can move beyond them in a way that is right for you. Only later, look at what you wrote and brainstorm some solutions.

Here's a tip. When you are brainstorming, never worry about "bad ideas." What you want is a free flow of all ideas because one leads to another, and you never know where your best will come from. Never censor your creative ideas. It's a process, not perfection, and the choosing afterward uses a different part of your brain that you don't want to bring in to interrupt the brainstorming!

Just remember, worry is stressful, and brainstorming is a release!

Down with Stress

Stress is tension caused by negative reactions to conditions or circumstances—absolutely no fun—and it is bad for you, physically and emotionally.

On a biological level, when you are stressed, your body releases hormones that flood your body with instructions on how to react to the threat—but that in high doses are actually toxic. Literally. It is why many people in highly stressful jobs don't live as long or stay as healthy as their peers. Stress is not excitement. Stress feels bad, but our society has somehow minimized and discounted its toxicity, and people endure it or manage it without looking at it clearly and solving the problem at its root. Stress is a hint or a clue that the situation is toxic and problematic. That is your cue to ask, "Why am I stressing about this?" and learn something about yourself.

Human behavior expert and coach Dr. John Demartini teaches that stress occurs when you compare something that is actually happening to what you wish was happening or think should be happening; you compare the two and find fault with what *is* happening.

That is important in actually negative situations, but stress can be a misfire when things are simply not going the way you want them to or you feel out of control. Or as author and innovator Byron Katie says in *The Work*, "The only time we suffer is when we believe a thought that argues with what is."

The first thing to do under stress and pressure is to acknowledge what is happening: "My boss is repeatedly upset." "I'm feeling the pressure of what I have to do." "I don't understand how this is organized." "I am repeatedly late to class and work." Acknowledge the truth. Then specifically create an active statement about the solution: "I want a good relationship with my boss." And decide whether you want to talk candidly to your boss or their boss, or you want to start looking for a new job with a kind, supportive boss. Be realistic and solution oriented.

Understand that if you simply endure stress—you live with it—you are telling your subconscious mind that the thing that is causing you stress is important. And of course, it may be important, but worrying or brooding over it isn't what's important; succeeding or solving the problem is the important part. So it is critical to a happy life to notice stress, acknowledge it, and figure out how to handle the situation from a calm, centered, and accurate place.

What if you are caught in traffic and ten minutes late getting to work, and you spend the entire time stressing about it? Or you are ten minutes late to work and you spend the whole time relaxed and accepting that you are ten minutes late? In either case, you're running late, but on the one hand, you are filling your body full of stress hormones, and on the other, you are calm, thinking clearly, and driving well. Which would you choose if you had a choice? Well, actually, you do.

There is a lot of material available on the internet and in libraries about stress management, and there is some in appendix 1, but briefly, when you are experiencing stress, deep and slow breathing brings your heart rate down and sends a signal to your brain that you are out of danger, causing the body to reduce levels of cortisol and adrenaline and allow relaxation. Moving your mind to thoughts of things you like and love—like pets and people—can initiate production of oxytocin, dopamine, and serotonin, which are often called our "happy hormones," and reduce stress. Also, spending time in nature—like walking in parks or by the sea, or even just sitting with your back against a tree—is one of the best-known ways to clear the effects of stress and support health and well-being.

Stress is physically exhausting. Please recognize when you are feeling stressed and take the time to breathe, walk in nature if you can, get a full night's sleep, and move toward the solution (rather than worrying about the problem) when you are able.

The Restorative Power of Sleep

Speaking of sleep, have you ever noticed that when you are sleep-deprived or exhausted, you often feel emotionally low or find that odd negative thoughts cross your mind? And then after a good night's sleep, the same things seem manageable; you wake feeling refreshed and normally energetic.

But when you were tired and down, did you believe that your gloomy thoughts were real? Most people believe the negative thoughts that come with exhaustion and fatigue. Next time you are feeling low, notice it objectively, but don't necessarily believe in it. If there is something of concern, write it down on page 1 in your 🎜*Workbook*, and then do something in the present that is purposefully helpful or cheerful, or take a nap, and go on with your day.

Sleep is critically important and undervalued in our society. We push ourselves without understanding the benefits of sleep or the harm in sleep-deprivation.

Take the time to make sure your bed is completely comfortable and welcoming. Pick colors and fabric textures you like, and then give yourself permission to spend eight hours a night regenerating and recharging there. Just like giving a full charge to your phone or computer. How can you love your life if you are burning the candle at both ends? If something wonderful comes your way, and you're exhausted and low in your mind, will you be able to enjoy it and make the most of it? Self-care is critically important, and it also feels good, so be good to yourself and support your best physical health, and that will influence your mental and emotional health. It's all connected. Each of us is one connected body, mind, and energetic self. I like to think of bedtime as spa time or me time, and I enjoy it. So often, I hear people complain, "I'm so exhausted!" as if it's cool or makes them important, and then I watch as it gets worse. I've learned to give myself a good night's sleep, and I feel so much better than I used to!

Understanding our thoughts and emotions is important for taking responsibility for ourselves and our reactions and increasing well-being in our lives.

Back to Positive Emotions, Have You Tried Love?

Speaking of well-being, please think of a person, place, pet, or thing that you love. Pick an easy one and think about it for a moment. Take a moment to feel your love for it.

Let both your heart and mind connect to the idea and feel the feeling of love. Love feels pretty great, right?

Now, imagine a future where each part of your life is full of the things you love—people, pets, places, work, play. Imagine that. For example, if you love bicycling and the idea of growing your own vegetables, imagine them exactly the way you'd love them to be in the fabulous life you are creating. You work in an organic garden with cool people all day, the produce goes to awesome restaurants in town, and you get off work in time to ride your bike home before sundown every day. *Feel* how you would feel if you could do the things *you* love for perfect pay, while helping large numbers of people who love it too. Imagine that! And the coolest part is you love doing things other people don't, and they love things you don't. If everybody did what they loved because it interested them or mattered to them, lots of important things would be taken care of by people who enjoyed their work.

When you *feel* what you are imagining, you are locking it in. You are teaching your subconscious mind that these good sensations are associated with that idea and they are important to you. Feel and think those thoughts over and over, and going forward, you will reactively experience more of that! So pick feeling good!

From now on, starting where you are, take the time to notice things that make you happy or make sense to you. Add them to your This Matters! list on page 12 in your *Workbook* and then as sentences on page 17 in your *Workbook*. Every time you write or reread them, feel great about them as you imagine and visualize them. Enjoy your plans and dreams!

Did you write down the things that matter to you in every aspect of your life? If your list is heavy in recreation or finances and low in the areas of family or health, your life will be out of balance! As part of *Building Your Best Life*, in the next chapter, we'll be considering all areas of your life to make sure it's all balanced in well-being!

On the inside cover of your ⌛Workbook, somewhere, in the right size and color, write one thing that truly matters to you—or any other words or designs that symbolize something that matters to you! And then write today's great date!

❧*W*❧

❧*Workbook Exercises for Chapter 4*

In your ❧*Workbook*, on page 11, you'll rewrite the positive statements from pages 7 through 10. Then reread them all and feel the great feelings that go along with them. From now on, read and feel page 11 daily as you bring about clarity and the shift you are creating. You are already on your way to your new, happier you!

In your ❧*Workbook*, on page 12, list ten or more important things that you care about on your This Matters! list. These are things that really matter to you, or that you think are cool, or that made you happy recently. Like all ❧*Workbook* pages, your This Matters! list will be active. Every time you notice something you care about or enjoy, add it to this page and take a minute to experience feeling really grateful for each of the things there.

In your ❧*Workbook*, on page 13, please begin or add to your Synchronicity List. Any time there is a synchronicity or seeming coincidence—or something shows up out of the blue that is just what you were talking about or needing—add it to this list. At first, these may not seem to happen very often, so just start your list. You'll see how odd it is that the more you notice them, the more they show up. They are the connecting of similar energetic frequencies, intentions, and experiences—where we can see our intentions manifesting, the *how* in process—and they often seem satisfyingly uncanny when they occur!

Chapter Five

Keeping It All in Balance

If you don't empower yourself INTELLECTUALLY,
you'll be told what to think.
If you don't empower yourself in BUSINESS,
you'll be told what to do.
If you don't empower yourself FINANCIALLY,
you'll be told what you're worth.
If you don't empower yourself SOCIALLY,
you'll be told what propaganda to believe.
If you don't empower yourself PHYSICALLY,
you'll be told what drugs to take.
If you don't empower yourself SPIRITUALLY, you
might fall for some antiquated model or dogma.
You are the one responsible for empowering all seven
areas of your life, in order to master your life.

—Dr. John Demartini, from his blog
https://drdemartini.com/blog/

The fact is true happiness, contentment, and fulfillment require balance in all parts of your life.

If you are unhappy in any area, you will feel and live that unhappiness whenever that part of your life surfaces, and it will spill over into other areas as you live your days feeling badly. If you are clear about all aspects of your life and make an effort to live in a way that feels right to you, contentment and feeling good are an automatic result. This is not to say your life won't have ups and downs. It's to say that in a balanced life, you will have the stability to handle your life and to live a life you love.

As we've explored, it is important to take responsibility for your well-being, and to notice and acknowledge what you are uncomfortable with or unhappy about. You then take steps to correct, accept, or eliminate it. Similarly, when you prioritize your comfort and happiness and take steps to secure them by making choices that take them into account, you are building a life of well-being. Maybe some of the things you do now or will choose don't make you actively happy, but they are important to you, and not doing them would make you feel bad. Those are just as important. We are not aiming for 100 percent happiness 24-7. We are building a stable, comfortable life full of the things that matter to you, and increased well-being will be one of several positive results.

So toward that end goal, let's look at a few more ideas.

The Areas in a Whole Life

Along the lines of what Dr. Demartini wrote in the quote at the beginning of this chapter, the areas or elements that constitute our whole lives can be looked at as family, friends and social interactions, creative expression, intellectual fulfillment, gainful employment, financial well-being, contribution, recreation, and health. We will be looking at what your life is like now in each of these areas—what you want to change for the better, what you would love to eliminate, and what you would love to add.

The objective is to acknowledge and begin to say *no* to the things that are less important to you or that you dislike and to say *yes* to the things that matter to you and interest you personally, in all areas of your life.

If you are persistent with the things you would love to have in your life, you are very likely to get them—or something better still. And by filling your time with things that you love, you will have less time for the things you don't enjoy, and your life will be filled with happiness and satisfaction. But you must keep it all in balance because if (for example) you overemphasize *recreation* and neglect *financial well-being*, you won't be happy. We will look at the things in these categories that you don't like or don't know enough about and figure out how to value or enjoy them and balance them properly for your happiness.

Defining All Areas of Life

For our purposes, the following applies:

- *Family* covers your relationships with your blood relatives and your chosen family if you are married or have a partner, as well as how you feel about these connections.
- *Friends and social interaction* includes not only what you and your friends do together but also how you are getting along, how happy you are with the company you keep, and whether you need more, less, or different friend time in your life.
- *Creative expression* includes personal projects, hobbies, and work that you love to do creatively.
- *Intellectual fulfillment* refers to the area of your interests where you feed your mind, learn and grow, and find out more about

things that interest you, which in turn helps you to become an intelligent and well-rounded individual.

- *Gainful employment* is where your income will come from so that you are self-sufficient.
- *Financial* is the overall picture of any and all income and assistance in respect to your financial needs, debt load, responsibilities, and goals.
- *Contribution* is what you can do to help make the world a better place, in alignment with your personal interests and values.
- *Recreation* is what you do to have fun or relax—that is, activity, entertainment, and socializing.
- *Health* includes physical, emotional, life force, and mental aspects of well-being.

There will be overlaps in most of these categories because we are a balance of all.

Relationships: Family and Friends

A good goal and intention for a balanced life is to find and surround yourself with people who understand, like, and respect you, and whom you enjoy, admire, and respect. It is important to have healthy relationships with family and friends, and with coworkers or classmates. It is important to clear up or remove relationships that make you feel unhappy. The way to begin this is by acknowledging the discomfort and addressing where the problem lies. In most situations, having honest conversations and the intention to improve the relationship works well. It can be hard to speak our truth, but try it out. Pick one small thing that bothers you in one relationship and cheerfully or kindly ask for what you need. Make sure they heard you, and then let it go. See what happens; that will be telling too.

In some cases, it is important to distance yourself from people who are hurtful or toxic. We'll talk more about this in the next chapter, "Cleaning It Up." And it is important to spend time with kindred spirits, people who get you and make sense to you. Sometimes we are so unique that these people are hard to find; then you just need to look harder and further. Reread your Interests List on page 15 of your ⚷Workbook. Chances are your kindred spirits will have some of the same interests, and if you find a class, group, or location where people practice them, you will make friends.

The human heart has a physical form and an emotional dimension, and research is finding that the heart is as much the core of our being as the brain. It is built to generate and experience positive emotions, including love, joy, and gratitude, and we are happier when it does! For more about that, check out the HeartMath Institute website research tab, listed in appendix 1. If you have friendship and love in your life, family and/or friends who love you—if you spend time around these people when it feels right and allow the good feelings to flow naturally while doing something constructive together—you can't help but feel happy while it's happening and a while after! A beloved pet works the same way!

In a real way, love is a key to happiness. Love is an experience and an emotion where your heart is activated and your body is happily producing feel-good hormones. So spend time actively loving what you do, what you enjoy, and being with the people who make you feel good. Romantic love is great when it's real, but it is not the only form of love. Real love is an emotion you feel when you are doing something meaningful or are with someone who matters to you greatly and is your true supporter. Unconditional love comes from deep within, and it lasts through difficult times. Often, we love animals unconditionally even though we have expenses and chores to keep them—showing that we may not like some things involving them, but we can still love them. Allow, seek, generate, and develop authentic love whenever you are able. It's a free flow, and it's healthy.

Be aware. If there is love in a toxic relationship, do what you need to heal it or distance and protect yourself. Just because you love someone does not mean you have to spend toxic time together. As an exercise, acknowledge what you have in common with the top ten people in your life, good or bad. List them on page 18 in your *Workbook* or on a handy piece of paper. These are your immediate family, friends, work or school associates, and so on. Do you share bad habits or negative outlooks with any of the main people in your life? For example, do you talk the same way about some group of other people as one of your parents or friends? Does your family nag or belittle, and you find you do too? Do any friends act superior, and you've joined in? And do any of your relationships with those main people need to be improved? For example, are you getting along with each person in your immediate family? Did you and your old best friend drift apart, and you're not sure why? Are things getting too tense with a coworker or teacher? Imagine the relief and better feelings if your particular situations were resolved! And which of those people are you happiest to have in your life—and why? Going forward, purposefully spend more time with them! Purposefully develop and enjoy shared interests. Do the things you both like doing, or stretch a little and make an effort to have fun doing what *they* like to do! Ask the same from them!

Creative You

You have imagination and original ideas, or perhaps you see things you like and make a new version the way you like it or in your style. Some people create music, some create art, some write, some doodle, and some imagine. Some people know what they love to do creatively, and some have no idea what they could do or would enjoy. Or, like me when I was starting out, some secretly feel creative but don't know their medium or abilities. To discover your personal creativity, here is another chance to notice what you notice. What creative mediums pique your interest? What do you stop to take in when you see them? If you can, over time, try those. Have some fun seeing what you like best! Remember that you are on a path. If you like something, give yourself permission to learn more and practice it. You may easily have several very fulfilling talents or trained abilities! These could be what you do after work to satisfy your soul, or as part of your fulfilling career, or something you do full-time! If art and music don't grab you, you might be a project creator, where your artfulness is invisible but the programs you create contribute to positive change. We all have creativity. It is a rich process. Hold the intention to explore and develop your own!

Intellectual You

Everybody has a mind and the ability to think, reason, learn, be objective, and question. Some people are highly intelligent, and using their minds is what they are interested in and where they excel. Some people need more information and experience to strengthen their minds. Your reading, listening, or studying and learning about what interests you is important for your mind, whether it is toward a career or a personal fascination. In truth, learning about almost all subjects can benefit us directly. It's all part of life on planet Earth, which is our playground! The more we know, the better we do at the things we love. Personal balance is the key. Our minds are important, and it's important not to neglect any part of ourselves.

Pick up or listen to a book on a subject or person that interests you. Read an article online. Take a weekend workshop. Go at your own pace and at your own level. This doesn't have to be daunting. It's interesting! Learning about the things that interest us and exploring subjects we know nothing about feeds our minds and strengthens the fabric of our lives. It enriches our perspective on life and subjects that interest us, cultivates curiosity, increases informed conversation, develops us as well-rounded people, and helps us discover kindred spirits!

I once took a class in economics because I needed the elective credit and it fit my schedule, but going in, I didn't even really know what it was and thought I'd be bored. It turned out that I was fascinated and dumbfounded by the complex understanding of how business, scarcity, abundance, and finances work! Who knew I'd be interested in that? You'll never know what life can bring if you don't open unexpected doors.

Again, this is about balance. You have a mind. Feed it and use it well.

Employment

Notice the distinction at this point between gainful employment and financial well-being. For our purposes, employment is work you get paid to do. You might have a job you love but that doesn't pay well; you might have a job you dislike that pays well; you might have a small job and be financially stable because of assistance; you might not be employed and need money to take care of your needs; and so on.

How many hours a day will you be at work? Full-time or part-time? Do you agree that if you have to work for money, you might as well enjoy what you're doing? We are creating balance, and if you need more money to do what you want to do, but you hate your job, that is not balance! There are thousands of jobs and careers to choose from, so take the time to learn about your options and work toward one you would love to do. It's often as difficult, and as easy, to get a job you'd enjoy as it is to get one you wouldn't. Employers in all fields need great, happy employees like you. Believe me, when I started, if someone had told me the odds of my succeeding as a film set still photographer, I would never have even bothered to try! If you are truly interested, determined, passionate, or committed, you'll make it or be led to a great match for you personally.

Every job has its ups and downs, so plan to have work that fundamentally interests you or contributes to the quality of your life. Even if today you have to take any job you can get, you can still start by applying to places that you can feel good about. And no matter what job you do, give it 100 percent while you are there. If you don't like a job you are in, figure out what you *would* like; then figure out what you need to do to be eligible for those jobs and take those steps. We'll work more on that in chapter 8, "What Is Your Calling?" For now, if you need more money to get training for a job you'd love, be thankful for the job you have that you don't like for giving you the money to live on and start saving! Feeling thankful about that while you are at that job helps you focus on your priorities, which will make it easier to endure! Whatever you do, be thankful for what you have and keep your focus on what you want. Author Jack Canfield goes into depth advocating feeling grateful as a way to enrich, balance, and improve our work, circumstances, and experiences, and Dr. John Demartini is brilliant on the subject of associating our values with our efforts to empower ourselves and strengthen our lives. See appendix 1 for their information.

Financial Well-Being

Generally, we get money from work, and we use money to live. Understanding our financial big picture is more than just finding a job and getting a paycheck. It includes managing the money-to-expense ratio in order to avoid unnecessary debt, paying yourself now into a retirement fund for later, how we feel about money, profit, and debt, figuring out how to combine incomes if you join with a partner, having and balancing accounting books monthly, all the details in homeowning expenses, the small print in bank loan contracts, the best way to help money grow in investment or an account, passive income options, and how to save for adventures. Those things and more are important to financial well-being, which is important to personal well-being.

For sure, money and finances are only part of our lives. Some people like money, some don't care, and some have bad feelings about it. We explored those perspectives a bit in chapter 2. Regardless, financial stability—with a lot of money or a little—is important to feeling comfortable, and it is important to understand that financial stability is well within your capability. You are capable, even if inexperienced. You need to have enough money for food and shelter, for fun, for your creative and intellectual interests, and to allow you to spend time helping others. If you have a job and you spend all your earnings having fun, you will face challenges with rent and groceries. Your intention must be aimed toward having enough money to be stable in all areas. Check out the books in appendix 2 for more information on financial stability.

Financially, there is now, and there is later. Let's start with now.

Current financial stability. Remember, you are like a radio; your thoughts and feelings have energetic frequencies and magnetic effects. If you constantly focus on what you don't have, or envy others, or feel bad about money in any way, those are the thoughts, feelings, and circumstances that you're perpetuating. Read that again.

To shift your circumstances for the better, start by being grateful for what you have, no matter how small. I mean that seriously. We can have a discussion of how it is hard or inaccurate to be grateful if you are really struggling, but focusing on the struggle is not the way to a solution, so for our purposes, it is not constructive (for more on the possibilities of gratitude, see Jack Canfield, appendix 1). Since what you focus on is what you will get more of, focus on everything working out well and appreciate what you have now. Start where you are now. Be grateful for what you have now. Enjoy what you have now. Each time you get some money, find a discount, or are treated to something, be happy about it! Be happy for what you have. Even though I am generalizing, I cannot emphasize this paragraph enough. This type of thinking has turned individuals with nothing into successful and secure citizens—over time and with inspiration and intention. Personal development specialists Oprah Winfrey, Lisa Nichols, Jack Canfield, Napoleon Hill, and many, many others go into detail about their personal experiences of going from having little to having enough (and more), and all describe that a positive attitude in the present and a forward-thinking perspective are critical to advancement toward financial and general well-being.

Next, notice without judgment what your financial needs are, and together we will plan how to have your needs met in the near future. If you are looking for work, first focus on jobs you would love to have and you know you would be good at; as I wrote earlier, they can be as difficult and as easy to get as jobs you don't enjoy, so start by focusing on personal interest plus income, rather than income only.

When you are considering your future employment, to the best of your ability, be clear on what actually interests you. If you are interested in amazing food or nutritious locally sourced ingredients, consider getting training as a chef, and meanwhile go to multiple appealing local restaurants and ask about entry-level support work. If you are interested in cool buildings or in neighborhoods being restored, plan on getting a degree in architecture or in community management, and meanwhile go to architectural firms and ask if they need help in the office. Pick people's brains, let them know you are looking for an interesting job, and ask their advice. See what suggestions are made that seem valuable, exciting, or fun.

If you are in school now, then school is the priority, and you may need to live frugally until you graduate; that's fine. You are not the first, and there are tricks and techniques. If you need a little more income and you feel you can spare a little time after classes, think about what you would enjoy doing and start asking the school administration and local businesses about part-time work; keep asking and searching until you find what you need. If you are a student with no extra time, speak to your family and the school administration about assistance. Or perhaps you'll have to take a quiet job, like a phone receptionist, where you can study between calls. The point is that if you hold your intention, look for work, and express your needs and interests long enough, assistance will appear. You have taken action and set the ball in motion.

Avoid credit card, payday, and bank loan debt if you can. People who don't manage debt well can get in trouble; however, taking on a small debt now—to make sure your basic needs are met—is better than functioning poorly at work or school. If debt is necessary, keep your perspective positive, be thankful and happy about the assistance, and start planning a summer job to pay it off—maybe with extra for you to save! Whether you are at work, looking for work, or in school, it furthers your well-being to appreciate what you have, notice what your needs are, and begin planning for what you would prefer. Try hard not to dwell on what you don't have or what isn't working well. Focus and act on the positive solution. For example, since eating out and going out for drinks quickly becomes a big expense, maybe avoid debt and expense by inviting people over, with everybody bringing something to share. There are creative ways to avoid and reduce debt, and you are a creative person!

If you notice that you keep hearing from others or telling yourself that you can't afford something, today is the day to shift away from focusing on what you don't have or can't afford. A scarcity mindset does not serve you, and it's often based on fear, not carefulness. If there isn't enough cash in the bank to buy something, don't sweat it; take a moment to actively appreciate what you'll make do with instead. If you are low on cash, *choose* not to buy it else rather than telling yourself, "I can't afford that." If there is not enough cash for what you need, then it is essential to get training for a professional skill that interests you or to look for work that pays better (always starting with jobs that seem interesting of course!) so that you can be gainfully employed.

There is a powerful phrase you might like using: *until now*. If you catch yourself feeling or speaking like you don't have enough, immediately say to yourself, "Until now!" and then keep going.

Future financial stability. Now let's consider your future five to fifteen years from now. Take a minute and imagine how you really want to live in the future. What does your home look like? Where is it? Do you live alone or with roommates or family? Are your friends living nearby? Is the recreation you love nearby?

Some people want small homes that are affordable and easy to lock up when they head out on adventures. Some people want enough room for the number of children and animals they would love to have. This is about you. What would you love? This will change and develop over time, but for now, let's work with how you feel now.

Please don't limit yourself to "I want to be rich." You can be rich and miserable; many people are. External possessions and circumstances don't inherently bring happiness. You can be unhappy with the same possessions as you can be happy with; the difference is in you, not them. Instead, imagine and visualize specifically what you want your future to include that feels good to you—a wide, comfortable bed, the right climate for your favorite recreation, happy family and pets, whatever seems great to you personally—and feel how wonderful it is to have it so. This is about you and *your* life. What you imagine must be specific and personal. In doing that, you are telling your conscious and subconscious mind exactly what is important (which, with repetition, has effect).

Imagine your perfect home and financially stable life, full in all nine areas.

Imagine each area in as much detail as you can. Who is there? How big is your home? Can you lock it up and leave for an adventure, or is it filled with animals and friends? Is it cluttered or clear? Near nature or in an active community? Enjoy the process of imagining it! See yourself there, happy! Again, instead of imagining "being rich," imagine having enough money to be comfortable in all areas of your life, including enough to share with and help others. A good life includes fulfillment, prosperity, and abundance in every aspect of life, not just financially. Your fulfilling life is not what other people think is good; it is simply what you will love.

No matter who you are, in the present, wealth and wealth consciousness are part of your mindset. Your mindset is what you believe and what you were taught, not necessarily what is true.

Whether you come from a financially stable, poor, or wealthy family, you probably think and believe in the way you were raised at home, in your neighborhood, in your society of advertisements and expectations. Whatever your personal situation, this is about you choosing what you want for your well-being. And this is not something to worry or stress about; this is something to intend happily!

Remember, intentions have energy, strength, and power. In most aspects of life, what you focus on is what you will get. So focus in detail on having enough, or, as personal development specialist Mary Morrissey puts it, "this or something better still."

Contribution

It is important to know or discover what you would like to do to improve the world around you. What do you care about? What matters to you? Some people care about how homeless families and stray animals are treated. Some people care that there is still poverty while at the same time there is waste everywhere. Some people care that by taking in stale air and carbon dioxide, and breathing out pure oxygen, trees and all other plants contribute directly to the health of life on earth. You will want to make contributions in the areas *you* care about, not to every outstretched hand.

Know that there are things that matter to you but don't seem important to others, so you are the shepherd and guardian of those things. And you may easily make great friends who share your interests. It is critical to understand that our contributions must be given with love and care; we all must practice happily giving and sharing. When you feel joy about supporting something that matters to you, giving is a natural overflow.

What do you wish you could fix in your town or anywhere in the world? What about contributing to a program that helps others participate in the recreation you love most?

Recreation

Recreation is what you do to have fun! It is anything you do for the pure joy of the experience! Often, these are things you like to do with friends who enjoy them too. You might love bicycle riding, watching movies, bowling, martial arts, walking in the mountains or at the beach, dancing, playing ping-pong or competitive darts, eating great meals in amazing restaurants, couples dancing, taking art classes, painting or sewing, playing sports or games, and so on. You might want to learn to windsurf or ride on a stand-up board, to play backgammon or chess. Fun and recreation are critical to happiness, and it is extremely important to create time for them in your balanced, happy life!

Do you keep a calendar, or is your schedule simple enough to know when you are always free? Pick a few hours every week that you can spare, and schedule them for a recreation you love. Don't give them up for errands or friends unless you are inviting your friends to join you! Remember, this is all about balance. I'm advocating you make time to balance in recreation, not to play so much it's conflicting with your requirements.

Since exercise is critical to health, determine what exercise you like, and whether it's bicycle riding, swimming, running, dancing, rock climbing, hiking, or body surfing, make it part of your fun and healthy recreational life!

Health

Our health is so important to our sense of well-being and to our ability to live with full vibrancy into longevity. And there are many aspects of our health: physical, mental, emotional, and our life force or energy body.

Physical health: Growing up, I heard the words "eat healthily" and "your body is your temple," and neither concept gave me the information I needed.

The facts are that your body has nutritional, sleep, and exercise needs to stay strong, ward off illness, and heal normally. And it's your job to care for its well-being. People often push themselves too hard at work, school, and in social situations, and in the long term, it doesn't work out well for their health and well-being. If you don't have good health habits, there is an important goal! Whenever possible, make it a priority to cook and eat fresh food (pick delicious things!), avoid preservatives, additives, fried and junk foods, spend eight hours in bed, and walk daily in nature if possible for at least forty-five minutes. Your body and mind will love you for it!

Your body is built to self-heal and carry you healthily for your whole life if you give it what it needs. Your whole self is integrated. If you don't get enough sleep, or you don't take care of your body in some other way, you will start feeling unwell, physically and mentally. For example, we do most of our restoring and healing while sleeping. Yet so many people drink too much coffee to mask fatigue, endure stress, grab fast food, eat and drink too much too close to bedtime, and then are exhausted and complain they don't sleep well. Most people just don't make the connection between their physical stress and their psychological outlook, and they start to suffer and believe their negative thoughts and feelings, which in reality are merely symptoms of exhaustion or depletion. News or not news—your body and mind are directly linked in health.

As an example of a good choice, I was working on a long, physical job when I saw a young coworker playing around with astounding agility. I stopped and asked her why she could even do that! And this is what she told me:

> My mother was a yoga instructor, which was a pretty unusual and unique thing in the mid-2000s in Southwest Ohio. My siblings and I were all type A, perfectionist athletes. All three of us also struggled with ADHD, and our minds were often as hyperactive as our bodies. My mother introduced us all to yoga when we were about thirteen, and it completely improved the relationship I had with my body and mind. Not only did it help me with flexibility, recovery, and injury prevention, but it taught me how to focus. Meditation seemed impossible and intimidating for an unmedicated ADHD thirteen-year-old girl, but doing yoga was a wonderful step in that direction. It allowed me to connect with my body and focus on the present, and I'm so grateful to my mother for teaching me those lessons so young. I've continued my practice into adulthood, and I notice and appreciate my physical flexibility and mindfulness every day. Especially when my sixty-three-year-old father eventually gave in and did a class with us recently. As

he fidgeted, looked around the room, and struggled to
touch his toes, despite being a healthy and active adult,
I realized how much starting yoga early benefited me.

If your regular recreation can include great exercise, bull's-eye!

Self-care: Nothing you do should be at the expense of self-care.
Whether at home, at work, or with friends, many people want to be
looked after and cared for by others. And some of us will do things
for our friends and family before we look after ourselves. Before
you look for someone else to care for you, before you take care of
someone else, learn to care for yourself well. Whose job is it to keep
your car running well? Yours. You have to treat it well and get it to
the mechanic if it needs it. If you neglect a pet, a plant, or your body,
you'll see and experience the results. If your goal is a happy, successful
life, accept that you need to make caring for yourself a priority. Good
nutrition, sleep, and exercise are your responsibility, so make it the
way you would like it!

Figure out what you love to eat and drink that are healthy. Notice
what it is about the less healthy food and drinks that you like. Is it
the extra sugar, salt, oils? Find healthy food with those qualities and
reserve fast food for once in a while, not for regular meals. Same
with exercise. Find what you like and make them part of your fun
recreational life. When we're young, good health seems normal, and
under normal circumstances, it is. But if you look at older people with
poor health, it is amazing what percent of their illnesses are due to
lack of self-care and bad habits that started young, to the point where
the body couldn't heal itself. My point here is that you can live into
old age with great health, and you will be much happier if you choose
that. As you consider and build the life you will love, good health
must be included.

A health sidenote: Anyone can be vulnerable to problems like negative self-image, negative self-talk, smoking, eating disorders, self-harm, and substance abuse (recreational or otherwise). If you are experiencing those, take care of yourself and get some help and support right away (see appendix 1 for some ideas). Please know now that those are all symptoms of difficulties occurring in the person's heart or mind. On the outside, they may seem okay, but hurting ourselves in any way is a clue that deeper down there is need for personal work so that the problems don't get worse or do more damage. Something happened or is happening that the person feels badly about or is deeply not okay with. Please know now that problems like these are all healable if the person acknowledges the behaviors and finds the healing method of choice (more in Chapter 6, "Cleaning Up Messes," and in appendix 1). We are built to heal on all levels; we may just need some help.

Substance abuse and eating disorders are not good for the body, and they can cause more physical and emotional problems in the present and future. We think we're strong, and we are, but we can damage our bodies and create health problems we'll have to deal with. I know firsthand that people caught up in these types of destructive behaviors will benefit on many levels by looking honestly at why they are inclined to act that way. In what situations are you more likely to do it? What are the feelings that go with it? Journaling is an amazing tool for that, and talking to the right person is important. See appendix 1. The good news is that when we address and heal the fundamental reason of why, in time, the symptoms fall away, no longer relevant.

If any of these are true of you, do not blame yourself in any way. As I've said before, blame and shame can be as destructive as any problem. They undermine us further. Know that you may not be responsible for what is going on, but you can take responsibility for taking care of it! It's important that each and every one of us gently looks at the root of our problems, instead of just enduring the symptoms or self-medicating them. Remember my story from chapter 1 of having the eating disorder bulimia as a teenager? When it was happening, I had no idea why. I hadn't even the faintest idea. I was just living the symptoms. With the help of a really great therapist, I figured out that I didn't feel good about myself on a deep level, because I believed my father didn't like or love me enough to stick around when I was little! That couldn't have been further from the truth, but I was still suffering from the trauma of my parents' divorce and believing that my father abandoned me because I wasn't valuable enough for him to stay around. I am so fortunate that I sought out and found that good counselor when I was in college. I caught the problem before it created lifelong physical damage and the psychological damage worsened. It's an example of how a negative self-image and childhood trauma can be very destructive, hurting us further both physically and emotionally. Sometimes these behaviors come because we feel out of control with our lives or to soothe an indecipherable sorrow. Our negative behaviors are a great clue to personal work needing to be done. The good news is personal work works!

Even if you or a friend are just hitting it too hard "having fun," if you are damaging your body, it's going to take a toll. Look at the older people who have been doing it a long time. Decide if that's what you want for yourself. And know that many things can start out fun or periodic, increase in time without you paying much attention, and then you find yourself doing too much. Always call it what it is, and don't let it go where you don't want to be.

We are working to build you a life you will love to live, so going forward, please intend that self-destructive behavior in any form is not part of it, while enjoyable self-respect and self-care are!

Our bodies hear our thoughts: Our body is also the product of the thoughts and feelings we have had, in part because they guide the actions we have taken. More than that, our thoughts and beliefs actually affect our bodies and health directly.

You may have heard of the placebo effect. It is described as the beneficial effect that takes place when a person is given a harmless and ineffective substance and is told it is something that will heal their illness, and then positive results occur. You have an illness, they give you a sugar pill and tell you it's medicine, and you get better because you believe you've been helped. The placebo effect is often thought of as a psychological pacifier or trick, and the fact that it works to heal the body was largely not understood and discounted in Western medicine until very recently. Many people still don't know much about it.

In fact, placebos have high rates of success. Do you know why?

Quickly, before we discuss why, I want to tell you that there is also a nocebo effect. When a doctor or other important person gives a negative prognosis (prediction), and the patient believes it, it can become a self-fulfilling prophecy. In his book *The Biology of Belief*, biologist Bruce Lipton explains,

> When the mind, through positive suggestion improves health, it is referred to as the placebo effect. Conversely, when the same mind is engaged in negative suggestions that can damage health the negative effects are referred to as the *nocebo* effect ... Your beliefs act like filters on a camera, changing how you see the world. And your biology adapts to those beliefs.

Just as a placebo can help us heal, a nocebo can cause our body to fulfill a negative idea that we genuinely believe to be true, as if the prognosis is a fact rather than a possibility. The things we think and believe, positive and negative, are creating our bodies' health. Our bodies hear our beliefs as instructions. So give your body what it needs to do well: nutrition, sleep, exercise, and belief in your ability to self-heal.

The important truth about placebos and nocebos is that they are not inert, ineffective psychological tricks; they show how the mind and body connection actually works. If you focus on a solution, if you believe in your body's ability to self-heal (which it is designed to do), if you know you can be well and are now on the path to get there, if you participate in healthy behavior like good nutrition, sleep, and exercise and address the cause rather than masking the symptoms, then you are telling your mind and body what is important and what to obtain. What you persist at in life, you will generally achieve; we only fail if there are equally powerful unresolved problems or external forces limiting us. Then we have to address those too! We can! Focus on figuring out those limiting forces in order to get them out of the way so you can move forward without false limitations.

Of course, there are physical conditions like losing a limb in an accident, or infections like strep and malaria that are caused by toxins or pathogens, which are intransigent qualities in the natural world. I am not so much talking about those as I am saying that in the majority of circumstances, our bodies are designed and built to heal. It is in our DNA. We *can* make a difference in our own health (even with strep and malaria), and it has been proven time and again that people have healed when their doctors could make the diagnosis and treat the symptoms but didn't have the answers to healing the illness.

Let's say you lose a limb you can't grow back. Well, then

acknowledge your sorrow and disappointment, allow and respect your grief, give love and acceptance to the surrounding area and to yourself, and then catch yourself if you find yourself dwelling on your misfortune. Instead, get grief help and save money for a robotic prosthetic, do physical therapy, buy cool clothes that fit, and purposefully go on with the things you enjoy in your life and with achieving your dreams. I don't mean to minimize the situation in any way. It is important to grieve, feel, journal, and lie low as long as you need to. But then isn't a positive adjustment better than living in a grief loop and not progressing past sorrow, blame, and disappointment? Many people stay with their sorrows for years because they don't know any better. I don't want that for you or for anyone.

Knowing this, going forward, let's focus on good health in order to create the actions and conditions to maintain it. Good health at all ages is a vital part of happiness and well-being.

A word about mental health: Our mental health is linked to, and as important as, our physical and emotional health. They are all intertwined and interdependent. Mental health is part of the balance that supports actual health. I go into it more in the next chapter, "Cleaning Up the Messes," and outline some resources in appendix 1. So here we will look at a few considerations to keep in mind as you sail forward.

Joy and laughter are medicine: There is an old expression—laughter is the best medicine. It's actually true that humor and laughter are great medicine for both emotional and mental health! It's not only the laughter; it's the accompanying absence of stress hormones, the release of health-inducing chemicals, the sound vibrations, and the joy you feel when laughing that support healing, processing, and well-being. If you were to make light of stressful situations in a cheerful way, or laugh at the irony and focus on the solution, you would be processing the stress and creating the shift toward resolution or improvement!

Close your eyes with a relaxed face for a moment. Feel what a softened, blank expression feels like—and then smile. Did you *feel* the difference? A physical smile brings a nice feeling with it! That nice feeling is literally good for your health! Did you know that giving someone a hug that lasts more than seven to ten seconds will relieve stress by producing oxytocin? And be careful. Just as smiling produces a cheerful and calming effect, frowning and scrunching our forehead triggers the release of stress hormones in the body!

If you are stressed about school or work or being late and you just stop, acknowledge it, and then smile genuinely—maybe even laughing at yourself for doing it again!—you shift your attention constructively. Make sure your breathing is slow, deep, and normal, and put your mind to the solution, change the subject to something that makes you happy, or put on some good music, and you will begin to shift away from feeling so stressed. It's our responsibility not just to manage our stress but to release it and shift to acceptance or resolution.

Some people purposefully watch funny movies, read comic writers, and listen to comedic podcasts as part of their healing routine. Some old comedy movies were very intelligently created. You can laugh, learn about the time in history, and enjoy good filmmaking for your health! Different things make different people laugh; there are so many kinds of humor. What do you think is funny?

Try purposefully and genuinely smiling and laughing as often as possible for three months and see the difference in your happiness and lowered stress levels. You'll start to feel it after the first weeks, but I'm suggesting three months in order to achieve and stabilize the benefits.

The ✍*Workbook*, page 3, number 7 is about what you think is funny, so read it, enjoy it, and add to it!

Down with stress: You definitely want to reduce your stress reactions. Many illnesses are stress related or are worsened by stress hormones. Feeling stressed and the release of stress hormones are caused by a negative reaction to something we see, hear, or experience. If we simply endure that stress for an extended time, suffering emotionally and producing physical hormones and muscle tension, our body will start to wear down, and we will experience physical symptoms to let us know that there is a problem.

Don't just live with symptoms, and don't just medicate them to suppress or cover them, or they can only persist and increase. As I've said, our bodies are built to heal, physically as well as emotionally. Even if a doctor doesn't know a cure or solution, that doesn't mean there isn't one. Our very first step is to intend to heal the problem that the symptom is signaling. Think only of discovering the solution; don't dwell on the problem. This strategy is beneficial for all problems in our lives, not just our health.

This is a principle we must understand and act on for health and peace of mind. Take the time to discover why you are having the physical reaction, whether it be pain, allergies, or exhaustion. For your whole life, to be happy, you can and must heal your health conditions through proper nutrition, sleep, appropriate exercise, proper medical assistance, and sometimes through psychological therapy, therapeutic body work, and energy medicine modalities (more in chapter 6, "Cleaning Up the Messes").

Emotional health: How healthy would you say you are emotionally? How much of the time do you feel happy, interested, courageous, compassionate, loving, joyful, thankful, appreciative, grateful, kind, caring, empathic, trusting, tender, and intimate? How often do you find yourself experiencing fear, anger, worry, phobias, trauma, self-sabotage, judgment, hate, betrayal, being lost, nervousness, sadness, shame, guilt, failure, humiliation, jealousy, and stress? We are built to be well, healthy, and happy, to accept things as they are, and to instinctively move away from harmful relationships and situations. If you find that you spend more time reacting negatively than you want, then I am very glad you found this book.

Some solutions to our emotional problems are described in chapter 6, "Cleaning Up the Messes." For now, just understand that your emotional burdens and your problems are with you now because they have not been processed completely and healed naturally on their own. Perhaps they just seem too big. You don't know how to deal with them, so you ignore them and push them down. That doesn't mean you are stuck with them. It just means you have not taken the time to do your personal work on them until they no longer carry repetitive negative charges for you. Perhaps you have not yet seen them as symptoms and clues of a problem. Once emotional burdens and problems are resolved, you will be wiser and stronger. It is well worth your time to address them completely.

What aspects of your emotional health do you wish were easier? If you haven't already, list those on page 4 in the 🍃*Workbook*.

Defining spirit and spiritual health: Before we go any further, I want to clarify what I mean here by *spirit*, *life force*, and *spiritual health*, and I don't want to get bogged down on this point or to offend anyone. I completely support what you believe or know to be true. I'm going to be addressing this subject periodically, so I want to use neutral terminology that you can read, understand in your terms, and feel as comfortable with as you would with any other concept we explore and consider.

By spiritual health, I mean the health of what people call the human life force, energy body, spirit, or soul. Whether you are part of a religion, or believe there is something out there you don't understand, or believe there is nothing but what you see, we can all agree that we have some energy that is present when we are living and is gone from the body at death. Author, healer, and teacher Deborah King explains it in her book *Heal Yourself—Heal the World*:

> This energy is a living force within you that originates both inside and outside of you. You may already know several names for it. The Hindus call it *prana*, the Chinese call it *chi*, and the Japanese call it *qi*. It's within you right now—invisible streams of get-up-and-go flowing through all of your body's energy channels or meridians.

So, when I speak about spiritual health, that is essentially what I am referring to, rather than a religious definition or set of beliefs— although our life force and the spirit that religions refer to may be one and the same.

Spiritual health: Our life force energy can become imbalanced just as the rest of us can, often occurring due to intense emotional stress. Balanced life force energy is a vital component of well-being. Our life force has function, connection, and purpose just as every other part of us does, just as every component in nature does. A healthy life force energy is as important as our emotional, mental, and physical health are. In fact, they are all connected and rely on each other.

So what supports healthy life force energy? Meditation, prayer, focused love, time spent in nature, and the earth's magnetic field all strengthen and balance our life force energy and keep us balanced energetically as a whole. An absence of those, and stress, can create an imbalance with symptoms including fatigue or lethargy, lowered immunity, and imbalances. Chinese medicine, acupuncture, therapeutic body work, energy medicine, and other energy work modalities work on this level. For more reading on the subject, see appendix 2.

Our health comes naturally if we take care of ourselves well.

Your Favorite Parts of Life Now and Intended

What are your favorite areas in your life today, exactly as it is?

And what do you love in each of the areas of your life? Family, friends and social interactions, creative projects or hobbies, intellectual interests, employment, financial overview, contribution, recreation, health? Add all those things to your The Things I Love list on page 16 in the &*Workbook*!

Today, being honest, which are the areas in your life that need more attention in order to seem good, balanced, and healthy? How would you love them to be?

Take a moment now. Close your eyes and imagine your perfect future again.

Remember that for a balanced life, it is important to take time in the present for the things that make you feel good—walks in nature, massages, meals with family and friends, alone time, and so on. When you do, you support your health and well-being, and you set up a future where time for the things that you love and that make you feel happy are a priority. When this becomes your practice, you love today, you are strengthening the foundation of your future, and you attract more circumstances and people that bring you joy and fulfillment in all areas of your life.

Practice doing what you love and loving what you do in *each* area of your life—finding the part of every activity that is meaningful or important, being aware of it, and enjoying that part as you complete your tasks. The more you do this, the more your whole life will start to fall into place, to feel good and right to you. Since true happiness requires well-being in all aspects of our lives, as you move through the circumstances of your life, consider the things you care about most when making decisions, knowing that if you are happy, you will do a better job.

Balancing our lives is not an exact science, and situations ebb and flow, with outside factors changing and other people having ups and downs. The point here is just not to overlook or ignore any part of your life or to have any part disproportionate. Think of the classic workaholic who spends so much time at work that their personal life is a neglected mess, or people who party so much that it's affecting their health and job. Give equal attention to all parts of your life when planning and making decisions, knowing you'll be happiest when all parts of your life are supported.

Remember your Make It Better List on page 1 of your ❧*Workbook* and your Unsure List on page 10? When you are building your best life, it's important to address the things that are still a little messy in our lives and look at ways to clean things up. Be it your kitchen or a relationship, in the next chapter, we'll be looking at cleaning up messes in order to create relief and balance and make space for bigger and better things!

On the inside cover of your ❧Workbook, somewhere, in the right size and color, draw a picture of a wheel with nine spokes, or a pie with nine slices. Maybe take a minute to figure out what nine equal pieces would look like before you use ink! We want the pieces to be roughly equal sized because we are seeking balance among all the nine parts of your life! And write today's remarkable date.

❧*W*❧

❧*Workbook Exercises for Chapter 5*

On page 14 in your ❧*Workbook*, list ten or more things you are good at on your Talents List. When you have ten or more listed, in the opposite column, you'll write one or more ways that that strength or talent can be used to help people. For example, if you have a good ear for music, you could become a DJ and play happy dance music, or an orchestra conductor so people have access to excellent, innovative live music. What are you good at? What can you do that your friends can't do or that doesn't interest them? No need to compare yourself; just accept it's your talent. Soon you'll see how all of our talents serve us and others!

On page 15 in your ❧*Workbook*, list the things that interest you. When someone talks about these things, what makes your ears perk up? If you were invited to do them, you'd say yes immediately. You think it is so cool that these things even exist! As you write, feel the feelings you would feel if you could work using some of those interests and make a living doing it! Imagine that, visualize it, and feel how good it would feel!

On page 16 in your ❧*Workbook*, write down the names of people, places, and things that you love. Take the time to feel the love for each thing as you write it. This is an important list, and we'll refer back to it, so take the time to name as many things as you can think of—people, food, places, fun activities, beautiful aspects of nature, animals, and so on. Later on, when you think of or experience anything else you love, add it to this list!

Chapter Six

Cleaning Up the Messes

This being human is a guest house.
Every morning a new arrival.

A joy, a depression, a meanness,
some momentary awareness comes
as an unexpected visitor.

Welcome and entertain them all!
Even if they are a crowd of sorrows,
who violently sweep your house
empty of its furniture,
still, treat each guest honorably.
He maybe clearing you out
for some new delight.

The dark thought, the shame, the malice,
meet them at the door laughing,
and invite them in.

Be grateful for whomever comes,
Because each has been sent
as a guide from beyond.

—Rumi, *The Essential Rumi,* translation by Coleman Barks

Ａll messes in our lives, great and small, sap our energy. How can we have and enjoy happiness when many things nag at us? How can we get up the motivation to actively pursue something that matters to us when we need to do, or are supposed to do, other things we have to but don't want to do? The truth is it's difficult to move forward when important parts of the past and present are a mess. Let's take inventory of your life in all the nine areas we just looked at, make note of where you have messes, and create the next simple steps to clear them up.

The Many Messes

Is your room or closet in disarray? Are the dishes neglected? Is your work desk disorganized, cluttered, or unwelcoming? Are your finances confusing or unattended? Is every part of your body as healthy and fit as you would love it to be? Have you made promises you didn't keep? Do you have family members, coworkers, classmates, or friends you avoid because you feel that there is something wrong with the relationship? Have you hurt someone? Have you hurt yourself? Have you neglected or avoided any obligation to your family, friends, school, or job? Have you started personal projects that now sit unfinished and subtly nag at you? Is something in your life going wrong or not going right?

We all have messes. But soon you will have a better balance, because today you can start cleaning up messes and making room in your life for what you prefer. Like the poet Rumi stated so eloquently in the quote heading this chapter, each mess is a guide. Something is unfinished because something about it is not right for you. It is time to take responsibility for your role in your messes and do the right thing in each, so that your heart, mind, and time are clear for what you choose to fill them with. This is gratifying work. As each unresolved area is completed, you will feel better and better, and that is where you are headed!

Cleaning Up Physical Messes in the House

Sometimes cleaning up physical messes is as simple as acknowledging that your trash can is ignored, your closet isn't big enough, you haven't allowed enough time, and you don't put things away when you are finished. These are practical organizational points that are easy and satisfying to resolve. If your current habit is leaving things out, you can absolutely shift over to the habit of putting things away when you are done using them, with the resolve that you don't want to leave unfinished projects that nag you, and no job is complete until it's cleaned and put away. It generally doesn't take much additional time! If you think something will take about fifteen minutes to do, give yourself twenty instead and clean up at the end! This is your life. How do you want it? When you clear up any mess, you make room for the positive things you are focusing your thoughts and intentions on. Welcome the clearing and enjoy the process of making things right!

For your home, set aside some time and plan not to be interrupted. Put on some good music; songs create moods. If you are into scented essential oils or think you could be, get an essential oil mister with something wonderful like tangerine oil for good vibes. Quite a few pure oils and blends are available online. Buy quality so the fragrances aren't artificial.

1. Get a big box and put everything in it that you don't need, haven't used, or doesn't fit and can be donated to a thrift store so someone else who needs it can use it.

2. Get a bag for any trash that is recyclable (recycling and reuse are critical to preserving the earth's resources and reducing unnecessary pollution and landfill).

3. Get a second trash bag and throw away all unusable and nonrecyclable items.

4. Put away everything that is lying out or set down where it doesn't belong.

5. If you don't have enough room for things, figure out if you need more cabinets or shelves or less stuff.

6. Now clean. Vacuum, dust, wipe down, and scrub.

7. Do you need to repaint?

8. What can you add to make the room nicer? Plants, glass that catches light, candles, essential oil mister, art on the walls, the right rug?

Make your space the way *you* like it, aesthetically plain or colorfully cozy. Make it look and feel great to *you* so that when you walk in the door, you relax. If you need to buy things to complete your space, choose only things that are both useful and beautiful. Pick colors and shapes carefully, to your taste.

Concepts for Happy Spaces

There are two concepts from traditional Chinese culture I'd like to explore here for home and work: feng shui and qi.

Feng shui means "the way of wind and water." Feng shui is an ancient Chinese art of arranging objects, buildings, and spaces to achieve harmony and balance; essentially, it is keeping spaces clear and making paths for the ways wind and water would naturally take through a room, home, and property. The result is a clear and open living or working space that feels nice to be in.

Qi, or chi, is defined as the vital energy of any living entity, and it is said that the flow of nature's qi must be unimpeded to maintain health. Free-flowing and healthy qi in the body is a central principle in Traditional Chinese Medicine and martial arts. The practice of cultivating and balancing qi in the body is called qigong. In the context of feng shui, it's understood that natural landscapes and bodies of water generate and direct qi through places and structures as part of the earth's universal qi energy—like breezes and water currents. There are many articles and books on feng shui and qi available online and in libraries, as well as advisers in some parts of the country (see appendix 2 for a start).

The idea is that you don't want to block the qi in your living or work space with clutter. Because qi has the same patterns as wind and water, a feng shui specialist who understands them can make suggestions in the home to affect these flows to improve aesthetics and circumstances. They can also show how to redirect the wrong flow of qi in spaces that, if not corrected, might bring bad results, such as stagnation, blocked emotional energy, blocked intuition, or the inability to stabilize wealth or health.

Holding these ideas in mind, the objective for you here is to make your spaces clean and clear to receive the healthy flow of life and good energy—the happiness and well-being that you are calling in.

Cleaning Up Your Physical Health

Where have you been neglecting yourself physically? Which aspects of your physical health would you love to improve? If you haven't already, list those on page 4 in your *Workbook*.

Physical health can be improved through the food we eat, good sleep, self-care, time in nature, and exercise. If you need to eat more healthily, find grocery stores and restaurants that offer food with delicious, healthy ingredients. If you can cook at home, buy healthy fresh proteins and spices and find your nearest farmers' market with produce grown in rich, healthy soil. Real food tastes great, so treat yourself to quality! Figure out what form of exercise you can enjoy or think is fun—like walking aerobically in your neighborhood on the weekdays, rock climbing, martial arts, qigong, or paddleboarding on the weekends. Do what *you* like and meet other people who like it too. If you have failing health, don't simply medicate to suppress the symptoms! Do the research to find the cause, and act to heal the actual problem. And allow time to sleep well on a regular basis. Spend the money to make your bed attractive and super comfortable, and spend at least eight hours a day in it, relaxing into sleep and stretching into wakefulness. As I've said, most healing and recuperation is done during sleep. That's what it's for. People say they don't have time for sleep, but believe me, they pay the price of fatigue that brings with it a negative outlook and less efficiency, and it can eventually lead to illness. I'm largely referring to people who stay up watching shows or partying and prioritize that above sleep. Yes, recreation and socializing are important parts of the balance, but no one ever told me how critically important sleep is to mental and physical health—that there are direct correlations. I thought I was invincible and pushed myself instead of prioritizing myself. I had to teach myself not to do that when I developed serious long-term exhaustion.

One of my favorite lines in Shakespeare is "Sleep that knits the raveled sleeve of care." Treat yourself to enough sleep, and you'll be happier! Your memory will work better too.

Cleaning Up Financial Messes

There are many great books and workshops on budgeting, saving techniques, getting out of debt, increasing income, income tax calculations, investing, and so on, so find yourself an interesting one in a bookstore or online (see appendix 2 for a start).

I had to teach myself to handle money and debt. I'm one of those people with little original mathematical ability or interest, so there was a high probability of my finances falling further into disarray than they did. I got caught in credit card debt and paid off only the interest until my partner stepped in, and together we paid off all my card and student loan debt in a couple of years. Then we started reading books on finances and investments. A point that stuck with me is that most people, poor to rich, feel that they do not have enough money. Part of it is mindset (the way they were brought up to think and feel), and part of it is a willingness to get into debt and to purchase beyond one's means. Western culture idolizes monetary wealth, and so many people compare themselves to those who have more. Even as people get richer, they often want more and more compulsively or greedily, instead of striving for a specific goal of enough and being content when you've reached it.

So after paying off my debt, we continued living frugally and putting the same payments into a savings account with the best interest we could find. When we had a bit set away, we invested in conservative, insured stocks and funds. When that grew, we used it as a down payment on the worst house on an up-and-coming city block. We lived in it and made it as nice (though not as big) as the nicest house on the street. We then rented it out for a reasonable income that was intentionally calculated to be more than all the house's expenses (mortgage, taxes, maintenance, and insurance). Five years later, we sold it at 50 percent profit, but as it was then considered an income-producing commercial property, we were taxed hard! We hadn't done enough homework to find out at what time we could have sold it more advantageously as a personal residence. We took the reduced profit from that, went through the same process again, and this time moved into it for a few years so it could be sold as a primary residence, which meant that the taxes in our state were far lower. At the end of that, we sold it for a nice profit.

I bring this up to show you that I didn't have an innate interest or ability with finances, but I educated myself, and you can too. Get out of debt, live at or below your means, save, pay into a retirement account (which means you are paying your future self some percentage of your current income each month), and keep debt levels affordable. In the future, would you rather pay $1,000 in rent to your landlord or have a $1,000 mortgage payment toward owning your own home? For now, clean up your financial messes and set your sights on having a modest home or condo you will love in the future.

Even if you can't think of buying or owning a home now, at least understand that there are ways to think and organize yourself financially that are helpful and manageable. If your goal is owning a home or a business, plan to take a financial management course or workshop so you have more tools to succeed (see appendix 2 as a start).

Cleaning Up Messes at Work or School

This is pretty straightforward. You have obligations and responsibilities. Fill them by giving 100 percent of your effort for a reasonable amount of allotted time. Don't burn yourself out or overextend; just do your best whenever you are working or studying. If there are subjects that are giving you trouble, find the people who can answer your questions, tutor you, or support you in doing things you don't do well (yet). If these are serious challenges for you that will continue into the future, figure out the easiest way to do your part or how to responsibly transition things that are not meaningful to you out of your life. Find a study program or a better-fitting line of study or work that supports your interests and values, something you'll enjoy doing day to day.

Remember, schools and jobs, like the rest of life, have ups and downs. I have a friend who usually likes her job but was recently miserable with two employees. It was so bad that she was upset every day at and after work, and she would call me for support. Her work problems were affecting her whole life negatively. She was on a deadline and on short notice didn't know of anyone to replace the employees. She is a great professional in her field and chose her priority of meeting her responsibilities and deadline above getting rid of them for peace of mind. After much stressful deliberation, she attached her value of professional integrity to the circumstance to get her through, knowing that when the project was over, she and the employees would part ways immediately.

And they did. It was a hard situation and choice for her, but since an easy solution didn't present itself, she weathered the storm and then worked with stress rehabilitation for a good while after that! She'd had several options—to fire them and hire unknown workers if she could find them and hope for the best, or to give up and let the situation fail because there were other people pulling it down. She made the difficult choice that seemed best to her under the circumstances. Life definitely has ups and downs. It is our priorities and responses that matter.

Sometimes you will have difficult choices and decisions to make. Sometimes there are unexpected ups and downs on the road to your goals. Keep your intention on what is best for you. If the rest of your life is stable and going well, you can handle fluctuations at work, school, and home. Balancing your life overall and relaxing after cleared-up-messes are both crucial to supporting your ability to rise to challenges.

Cleaning Up Relationship Messes

How much power do you actually have as a young person in your relationships? Do you feel like there are things you can't do because someone else won't let you? It's important to acknowledge that, and then it is important not to stay stuck there.

You have a voice—every human does—and if yours is suppressed for any reason, acknowledge that, notice when it is hard to speak up, add it to your Needs Improvement List on page 4 of your ☙*Workbook*, and write what you would love to have instead on page 5 of your ☙*Workbook*. All you can do is take care of yourself and take responsibility for your part in any given situation. You have to do what is right for you and do it in a way that is respectful to others. Let's say your relationship with a family member is a mess because of how they behave. Well, today that is so. And then how do you act when they act like that?

Your reaction is your responsibility. Find a moment to tell them clearly, from a grounded, stable place at a calm time, what you think and want. Or go to a different friend, family member, or professional counselor, adviser, or coach and tell them. Author, teacher, and healer Deborah King encourages people to go talk to people who aren't involved, advising that it produces a cleaner outcome. That is excellent advice when possible. If you talk to one friend about another, or one family member about another, it can get complicated and messy.

Visualize your life with that problem relationship resolved or, if necessary, finished. Again, don't settle for what you wouldn't choose for yourself. If you don't have the power to change it constructively now, intend what you want for your future and take any step toward that that you can.

It's important to see what your part is in experiences or relationships that you don't enjoy. Maybe someone is argumentative, and you react by arguing back or by becoming hurt and withdrawn instead of calmly standing up for your truth to see what shifts may occur. Recognize that you are part of your current circumstances, even if you feel that the other person started it. Even if you feel something is happening *to* you, you are responsible for your response. If something in your life is bothering you, don't simply endure it as if it's just the way it is. Resolve to repair, accept, or eliminate it and start the process of addressing it. Learning this early in life will have a bundle of benefits!

In his blog, author and motivational coach Jack Canfield (https://jackcanfield.com/blog/) describes it this way:

> If you want to create the life of your dreams, then you are going to have to take 100% responsibility for your life as well. That means giving up all your excuses, all your victim stories, all the reasons why you can't and why you haven't up until now, and all your blaming of outside circumstances. You have to give them all up forever.
>
> You have to take the position that you have always had the power to make it different, to get it right, to produce the desired result. For whatever reason— ignorance, lack of awareness, fear, needing to be right, the need to feel safe—you chose not to exercise that

power. Who knows why? It doesn't matter. The past is the past. All that matters now is that from this point forward you choose—that's right, it's a choice—you choose to act as if (that's all that's required—to act as if) you are 100% responsible for everything that does or doesn't happen to you.

If something doesn't turn out as planned, you will ask yourself, "How did I create that? What was I thinking? What were my beliefs? What did I say or not say? What did I do or not do to create that result? How did I get the other person to act that way? What do I need to do differently next time to get the result I want?"

It's important to note the *difference* between the ideas of *taking responsibility for yourself now* and *being responsible for having caused something* and blaming yourself or feeling guilt or shame. You can ask yourself what your part was if it is useful in creating change, but the bottom line is that this is not about whose fault it is; rather, it is about taking responsibility for yourself now and getting to where you will be happy.

Are there people to whom you owe an apology? An apology is defined as an expression of acknowledgment, remorse, or regret for having said or done something that harmed or upset another. In the twelve-step programs (which were originally created to help people with alcohol or drug problems but now cover many other issues), apologies are treated like this: "Step 8: We made a list of all persons we had harmed, and became willing to make amends to them all." This is seen as an extremely important step in the process of mental and emotional healing and health. Sometimes we're not able to apologize directly to the person because it isn't safe or they are no longer around, in which case—and in all cases—we must fully forgive ourselves. It's very helpful to journal your apology or to imagine the person in front of you and apologize in all the detail you would if you could.

Self-forgiveness is a crucial part of mental and emotional health. It is coming to understand that you made a mistake, and while not necessarily accepting the result, you accept that it happened—and apologize to yourself as well as others who were affected if possible. There is a powerful and ancient Hawaiian healing modality called Ho'oponopono, which teaches the value in expressing apology and gratitude (said silently or aloud): "I'm sorry, forgive me, thank you, I love you" (see appendix 1 for more details).

Blame Is Focus Outward

As adults, every time we blame others for hurting or disappointing us, we are looking at them (so not at ourselves). In fact, their problems are not our responsibility. It's not up to us what they *should* do. Clean up your relationships by cleaning up your part.

Why do we blame? Why do we focus on them and their actions or faults? It's good when we are assessing truth and calling something what it is. But when we blame the other person, it puts the focus outward, and then we aren't looking at ourselves for things we need to do or at ways we can do more for ourselves. It is so much easier to blame others than to look at ourselves, but when we look at ourselves, we take back our power.

I remember in a certain relationship, it was not until I stopped blaming the other person and focused on myself in the problems of the relationship that I gained the power to speak my truth and change the dynamic. It was a remarkable experience going from feeling wronged to doing something on my behalf! In effect, when I was blaming, I lived with the ongoing problem because I was focusing on wanting the other person's behavior to change.

Maybe the other person or group didn't behave well. *Regardless*, as an adult, what was our reaction? Not to assign blame but to ask ourselves, "Was my response what I would want it to be? Was I irritated, and the other person felt it and responded in kind? Did I have inaccurate expectations, so the outcome was disappointing? Was there a personal truth I didn't speak up about or stand up for in a calm, firm way? Did I not walk away or get help when I needed it?" You aren't looking for self-blame or fault here; it's just a chance for objectivity and to consider how you would prefer to respond. It gives you agency, while blaming the other person doesn't.

Please don't spend your precious time, energy, or focus on blaming yourself or others or faulting the system. Notice what you don't like and then take action to produce the outcome that you actually want. Don't blame and don't complain about others or the news. If you do, you are increasing the time in your day that you spend being unhappy, and that is unhealthy for you and those around you. Choose to do something or let it go. If it is bothering you, take a long walk, journal, or call a friend to talk about how you feel in order to process and resolve it.

If you need to speak up for or request change, do it without including blame. Your points are stronger if they are kind, constructive, and about what you *do* want.

You are your responsibility, so stay focused on *your* intentions, needs, and objectives. Speak your truth when you can. It's uncanny how personal truth becomes the strength you can act with. If you are unhappy about something, notice it, accept that at that moment it is playing out the way it is, and act toward the solution.

You're in Charge

We can all look at our past and see how as children we were not in control, and we may still be involved with some relationships that way. Look at your relationships and know now where you stand and what you want. Imagine your life the way you want it. Make your own constructive plan and write down the first steps needed in that direction on page 9, number 4, in your ♣*Workbook*. When you catch yourself in that relationship, not enjoying it, acknowledge that and assure yourself "until now." Then do one or more constructive things toward the shift.

Sometimes there are things going on in our families that feel unbearable. It has happened to many, many people. Some people you see daily are going through it and hiding it. The thing I want you to know is that there are healthy alternatives even if you don't see them now. Let me assure you that recreational drugs, alcohol, and other unhelpful behaviors don't change the problem; they just mask or cover your seeing and feeling it. Know that, in general, depression is a symptom that something else is wrong in your life. It is different for each person and not an isolated reality in and of itself. The key is for every one of us to take care of ourselves now and look for constructive alternatives or outside help. It may take the form of a certain family member, friend, mentor, counselor, coach, healing arts worker, or therapist; all these people are there for the exact reason you need them. They are resources.

Cleaning Up Mental and Emotional Messes

If you have personal problems and stresses, please know that most people do. Some live with them, and some people do the work to heal. Please decide now, with me, to resolve your problems rather than enduring them, and we will look at ways to do that personal work. You can and must do your personal work in order to heal back to your centered, authentic self. Healing can be a relief!

I am truly sorry if something terrible happened to you, whether in your childhood or more recently. I mean that. You didn't deserve it. Please know that just because it happened doesn't mean it has to define you. You are you, not what happened, so let's go forward with you.

Instead of staying in the pain as if it is your only option, you can do what I refer to as personal work. You can learn from what happened and become a stronger person, you can help other people who are going through it, and you can heal and get past it so it is just a memory—instead of your problems working like a filter, coloring what you perceive today. When we process our experiences in a healthy way, we get past their negative grasp on us. Then they are only in our memory, not a trigger or trauma anymore. If thoughts and situations trigger and upset you, know that you are not alone and that you simply have some personal work to do. Have a look at appendix 1 for ideas if you are interested in working to support and accelerate healing.

Many people put their upsetting memories and feelings into some mental closet, trying to ignore that they ever happened, but even if they actually forget them, they still color their perceptions and sap their energy. Suppressing upsetting memories is a survival strategy, but it isn't healing. Sharing troubles with a nonjudgmental confidante or counselor, a calm and sensible person who can let you bring the memory into the light, can help you release old pain, shock, or anger. Please keep working on healing yourself until you can think about the occurrences in your life as factual rather than reexperiencing your pain or other reactions.

There are people devastated by lesser things and people who have healed, balanced, and succeeded with happiness after much worse events. The difference is their understanding that they can feel better and their fierce commitment to doing so.

Problems are symptoms of personal work needing to be done. As Rumi said in the quote that opens this chapter, they are a guide. For example, eating disorders like bulimia and anorexia are symptoms of something going on in the person's heart and mind. People with those conditions, and all personal problems, would genuinely benefit from facing the *why* and getting to the bottom of it.

As I said before, when you address and heal the fundamental reason, the symptoms fall away, no longer relevant. The same goes with drug or alcohol abuse. Look to the root of the problem. Don't just live with the symptoms, justify them, or medicate them. Instead, get some help and support (see appendix 1 for some ideas).

Self-Talk

One of the first messes to clear up for your emotional and psychological well-being is to stop any negative self-talk like "I'm so dumb," "I'm ugly," "I'm bad at that," "I'm weird," and so on. These thoughts are not truths; they are mind chatter, criticisms, and limiting beliefs.

Every time you tell yourself anything negative, you are literally damaging yourself unnecessarily. Every time you catch yourself doing that, please, simply notice it, interrupt it, and change the subject of your thoughts. Every time. Seriously, what is the point of it? What is it good for? It's a habit, not a tool or great way to live, so please decide to stop today.

This is important for several reasons, a vital one being that you begin to believe what you tell yourself repeatedly, including things that are simply not true, and it can be weakening and damaging. If you compare yourself to someone who is taller than you are, and you tell yourself you are short, you won't feel good about yourself. And they may be comparing themselves to you and feeling bad that they're too tall! So you both feel bad for no good reason or outcome. There is no good or bad with height, and there are pluses and minuses to everything in life! You are the height you are. Period. Accept it. Rock it. Don't bother to judge it. If brain chatter says you are too anything, notice it, interrupt it, and change the subject of your thoughts. Take care of yourself. Be good to yourself. It will pay off in ways you can't imagine yet.

If, as another example, you say, "I'm bad at math," that becomes an instruction, and you will most likely give up before trying to get past that. Instead, if you link math to what you are interested in—"I want to work on oceangoing ships, and I need to understand how to budget to afford my training, and how much I'll need to earn to support the lifestyle and retirement I want"—then when you are in an accounting class, you will have an interest in the subject and will realize you can handle it if you put in the effort!

Maybe you'll need extra tutoring. So what? It might be easy for some people and more difficult for you. So what? Put your mind to it, and you'll get further than if you start by telling yourself, "I'm not good at math." Believe me, there are people who are automatically good at it, who won't bother to try hard, and who will end up falling behind or not trying, while you end up with the information you need for your great life! And this is true of everything. You get back what you put in.

Similarly, if at some point you don't feel good-looking, don't let negative self-talk tell you that you aren't—ever. Notice the thought, interrupt it, and think of something else purposefully. Then, if appearance matters to you, purposefully do something that feels right to you, like getting a cool haircut, going thrift store shopping and choosing clothes that fit your character, buying the kind of jewelry you like, or purposefully eating food that is better for your body.

Just do your best and accept where you are now with the intention of getting to where you would prefer to be. That's all a person can do, and it works.

If someone else tells you anything about yourself that is not constructive, don't buy into it, *even if it matches something you have already thought about yourself.* Remember, even if there are other people who are automatically good at something, you can still learn more about something than you know now and end up with what you need for your great life.

Words Matter

Every new thought creates the potential for change, and every repeating thought reinforces and perpetuates an existing perception. Your thoughts create your life. No one ever told me that.

Blaming and belittling words carry impact, just as kind and loving words do. Begin noticing how you speak—and how others speak around you and to you—and take responsibility for your words, good and bad. There is a communication technique called Nonviolent Communication by Marshall Rosenberg, which clearly explains that if you say things like "You're such an idiot!" even jokingly, on the surface it means you don't agree with them, but it's effectively a put-down and disempowering. And if it's said in anger or with irritation, it's more than an insult. These days, people act like speaking sarcastically doesn't matter—like "Wow, that was really smart," when you make a mistake—but it really does matter. The meaning is clear.

People start to believe what they hear repeatedly, especially if it resonates with an area of weakness, and self-doubt can deepen. When you are trying to clear up messes with people or with yourself, be really clear on, and with, the words you use.

Also, there are words like *try* and *want* that are limiting forces unto themselves. "I'll try to help" allows that you may not succeed fully. "I'll help" is a different concept. "I've always wanted to learn Spanish" can leave you wanting to learn Spanish for years but never getting to it. "I'm going to learn Spanish" and "I've decided to learn Spanish" are clear instructions to your mind and more effective for actually achieving. Don't just *try* to clear up your messes. Don't *want* to. Clean up your messes.

Monkey Mind

Most people have what is called monkey mind, where our mind runs with chatter, invasive thoughts, worry, and random ideas about our lives. Monkey mind keeps people up at night and invades their days. It is important to notice when your mind is running and to notice other people who live caught up in their running mind. Aware of this, it's important to have the objectivity and awareness to let those chattering thoughts go by instead of indulging or believing them. Just because you thought something doesn't mean it's true. We must all notice if our mind is racing, then slow it down and steady it. We mustn't allow our minds to be a ceaseless spring of concerns and worries. Journal those worries when you can, talk to a friend or professional, or take walks in a park or nature when you need to regain balance. But in the moment, don't let your mind cycle negative thoughts. Notice it's happening, acknowledge it, and shift your focus to something actually taking place in the present. Meditation is a great way to address monkey mind and teach the mind to pause and be present rather than generating chatter. More on meditation in chapter 10.

When Bad Feelings Get in the Way of Moving On

There are many ways to address and heal your personal problems, but it is important to understand that enduring them does not solve them. To heal, you must find a supportive, comforting way to fully face what has gone wrong for you and to process all the negative feelings and ideas until the negative charge is gone and the information becomes a mental fact, not a recurring emotional upset.

Believe me, this is possible, and people have recovered solidly from depression, abuse, grief, and severe personal problems. But to heal emotionally and mentally, you must be active in your personal work and growth.

Author, teacher, and healer Deborah King had an extremely difficult childhood, yet during a workshop I attended, she said what has become one of my favorite quotes: "When I can laugh at my problem while looking at it in the rearview mirror, I know I've made progress!"

We all must choose health and strive for it. We are designed to heal; we just need help sometimes. Here are a few methods you can explore for emotional healing:

- twelve-step groups, including CoDA (relationships)
- accelerated experiential dynamic psychotherapy (AEDP)
- acupressure and acupuncture
- Ayurvedic medicine
- Byron Katie's The Work

- chiropractic body balancing
- Discover Healing's Emotion Code and Body Code
- DNA reprogramming course by Annaliese Reid
- dream analysis
- Emotional Freedom Technique (EFT)
- eye movement desensitization and reprogramming (EMDR)
- grief support groups
- Hawaiian Ho'oponopono
- healing coaches
- Heart-Math Institute Heart Coherence practice
- holistic nutritional therapy using diagnostic muscle testing
- holistic Traditional Chinese Medicine
- journaling
- medical and healing qigong
- mantra-based meditation
- Neuro Emotional Technique (NET)
- reflexology
- reiki
- shamanic energy clearing
- shiatsu bodywork
- talk therapy
- talk-therapy groups or workshops
- transformative body massage
- yoga for stress reduction and mind calming

Please see appendix 1 for details, and of course the internet has more options and information.

When it comes to practitioners, sometimes it's hard to figure out who to work with, but use your good judgment and trust your instincts to find one who feels right to you. The person needs to feel like a good personal match to you, as well as a good listener who shares relevant observations.

Used correctly, healing modalities soothe and calm the nervous system, reduce excess stress hormones, process negative energy, increase your production of healthy hormones, improve the flow of blood and lymphatic fluid, and support healthy sleep (during which most healing occurs).

These are all different paths to the same place—a healed, balanced, authentic, and happy you. Don't knock any of them until you have tried them with a great teacher. Some of them will seem good to you, and others won't, and that's because you are unique. Please don't let other people, unfamiliarity, or social stigma get between where you are now and what you want for yourself. There are many great personal work options. Find out what is available in your area and online. A great teacher in a less interesting method could easily be more helpful than a mediocre practitioner using your method of choice, so be open!

Cleaning Up Your Life

In every case, treat others as you would want to be treated. Wish others well. Keep your promises. Keep your cool and your integrity. Mind your own business and stay in your own lane—but do let others know if you'd like to help or support. If there is something going on that you don't like or aren't comfortable with, respect how you feel and either speak up honestly or step away if you choose to.

If things are not going the way you want, become better, not bitter. Notice how you are feeling and reacting, and if there is a negative component, acknowledge it and take action toward the resolution that feels best for you.

As you clean up your messes, think about the clear space you are making for the good things you wrote in your This Matters Statements on page 17 in your ❧*Workbook*. Read that ❧*Workbook* page again now. Feel how good these things are! That is where you are headed! Onward!

In the next chapter, we will explore beliefs that might be blocking you from building your best life and practical tools and techniques for overcoming obstacles.

On the inside cover of your ❧Workbook, somewhere, in the right size and color, draw a crazy tangle, like a ball of knotted string, with one end clearly coming out and heading forward. And write today's good date!

❧ W ❧

❧ *Workbook* Exercises for Chapter 6

On page 17 in your ❧*Workbook*, you'll write positive statements about each of the things on your This Matters! list from page 12 in the ❧*Workbook*, as if they are now fully and fabulously in your life! For example, if you had "growing my own vegetables" on your list, you'd write something like, "My garden is so full of ripe vegetables that my friends come over, and we harvest and cook dinners together." Fill out these sentences describing exactly the way you *want* things to be in the fabulous life you are imagining and creating. Remember, when you feel what you are imagining, you lock it in, teaching your subconscious mind that these good feelings are associated with that idea and are important to you.

On page 18 in your ❧*Workbook*, you'll make a list of the main people in your life. Put a check next to the relationships that need to be improved and write why. Put a star next to the ones you are happiest to have in your life and write down why. Going forward, purposefully develop and enjoy shared interests and time with them!

On page 19 in your ❧*Workbook*, list the messes in your life today. If you have trouble finding messes in any area of your life, look back at page 4 in your ❧*Workbook* and add them to page 19. Then you'll look at how you make each situation right for *you*.

Chapter Seven

Overcoming Obstacles

You must build yourself in such a way that when opportunities open up in your life, your body and mind will not hold you back.

—Environmentalist and yogi Sadhguru, from his app's daily posts

On your path to the life you'll love to live (as you described excellently on page 9 in your *Workbook*), you will certainly encounter obstacles, which you can resolve and grow from. Obstacles and challenges are part of life. It's how we respond to them that matters.

I surely had to overcome many obstacles in my career! I remember when I found out that to work as a Hollywood film set photographer (taking photographs for publicity, advertising, and archiving), I had to be in the International Cinematographers Guild, and to join, I had to work one hundred days on nonunion films where I was the official unit still photographer listed on the call sheet, then pay $5,000 that I surely did not have and couldn't imagine getting. Believe me, those seemed like unsurmountable blocks. Having no contacts or leads, I just hunkered down and was determined to get those hundred days by calling people I didn't know (cold calls)—and I did it! I took the leap and scraped the money together from earnings, borrowing, and credit debt. It was frightening turning that money over just because I wanted to have that career! Almost immediately after, from another cold call, I got a two-week job at union-scale salary and earned exactly $5,000 on that job! I was cheerful, hardworking, respectful, and grateful. I took a calculated risk with no guarantees, but I'd say in that case, Providence moved on my behalf. There were so many other obstacles along the way I can't count them. But I never let one defeat me. I'd cry or curse in private and then figure out what I could do next to keep going.

Many people consider obstacles to be stop signs. They are not. Do you think fear is a real stop sign? Are doubts, the word no, or other people's resistance to your change (or to things they don't understand) actual stop signs? When you come up against something you perceive as blocking your path, stay focused on your good goal and work around the obstacle, resolve it, or find another way to get where you are going.

Let's say you apply to five jobs or five schools and you don't get into any of them. Do you stop there and tell yourself, "Well, I guess it wasn't meant to be"? Not if you want it badly you don't! You apply to five or a hundred more until you are accepted, and then wherever you land, you give it 100 percent and come out on top. Make the effort to determine why you didn't get into your first choice, and while succeeding at another, you could even reapply to the first! Commitment and persistence are attractive and powerful when communicated with goodwill and enthusiasm. If you never get into your first-choice program, excel where you are and don't look back. Later, use the same persistence in looking for employment.

Do you feel blocked from getting what you want in any area of your life?

Try Another Perspective

If we want change for the better, we need to begin thinking differently. We got to where we are now by thinking the way we think now. A great place to start changing directions is by looking at the obstacles of doubt, fear, and uncertainty. Often, we can't do more within the limits of our thinking, so we need to begin to see things with more objectivity, more wisdom, and less reactivity. It's been said that you can't solve problems with the same thinking that created them. In order to get where you want to go, it is time to rework your thinking and beliefs about obstacles.

Trust Your Instincts

In his book *A Path with Heart*, Buddhist author Jack Kornfield wrote, "I set my intention to allow my subconscious mind to speak to me, and things will happen exactly how and when they are supposed to."

This is a great affirmation, and I say it to myself every morning. This is about being aware of what is happening around you and how, although life in the present is the product of past thoughts and actions (by you and those around you), the present moment is also open to Providence.

It is important to learn not to judge everything that appears blocked or doesn't feel right as bad or wrong. If you don't like something, look at it closely and see why. It's important to trust your instincts; if it doesn't feel right, acknowledge that and take care of yourself and others. But also recognize that if you are reacting from unhelpful, old ways of thinking, and you have clearly committed to change, you may meet some resistance on the way—inner resistance to change and resistance from the people around you who don't share or understand your dreams. Resistance can be an obstacle, or it can simply be seen objectively as part of the process of change. Life doesn't always go the way you planned; that is normal and not because of a personal failing. Again, it is how we respond to what life brings that is our responsibility.

Obstacles Are Guides

Maybe something that isn't right for you will persist because it is all your subconscious mind knows, like a bad habit, self-blame, or discouraged thinking, because that thinking used to be repeated in your life. Look at every obstacle as a guide. Is this part of the past you are evolving out of, or is this an indicator that something is not in alignment with your goals and intentions? For example, if you disliked school, got poor grades, and then applied to highly competitive schools, you might not get in; your past perspective or circumstance is out of alignment with your current intention. In that case, do you give up? Is that a stop sign? No, it isn't! What if you start focusing on what it takes to get great grades now—summer school maybe?—and write the most amazing essay about *where you are today* and where you are heading, recognizing that there is a chance you'll have to start at a less desired college and reapply to this one or find a different college that is amazing in other ways. Think outside of your box so that you can climb out of it!

Similarly, what kind of person do you think a good employer would prefer to hire—somebody who is super-good at their job and highly experienced and intelligent but has a bad attitude and isn't happy, or someone who's interested, dedicated, wants to learn and be trained, enjoys what they're learning, and is committed to the prosperity of the business? Don't be afraid to ask! Find out what your dream job requires and become all that and more.

Solution Techniques

On a practical level, there are business and personal coaches who have written books and/or consult with clients on how to overcome obstacles in the workplace, in families, and in any other group decision-making. You don't have to figure out everything yourself. Support is available!

In his book *The Success Principles*, American best-selling author and coach Jack Canfield describes basic rules for succeeding in what you set out to do and shows how anyone can follow these principles to achieve their goals. He clearly outlines his own path to personal and financial success, sharing ideas you can apply to any part of your life where you feel you are facing problems.

Another method of problem-solving comes from Maltese psychologist, author, and inventor Edward de Bono, who teaches that if you take a problem apart and evaluate it from different perspectives, one step at a time, the answers will become clear. In his book *Six Thinking Hats,* De Bono suggests the following:

* Green Hat Thinking: Generating creative ideas and brainstorming
* Red Hat Thinking: Exploring feelings, hunches and intuitions
* Yellow Hat Thinking: Looking at all the positive aspects
* Black Hat Thinking: Considering all the negative aspects and cautions
* White Hat Thinking: Listing all the actual factual information available
* Blue Hat Thinking: Organizing, summarizing, and drawing conclusions

This technique works for one person trying to figure out a problem or for a team. You can see that in any group, if one member is stuck in positive thinking, another in creative brainstorming, and no one is considering the downside or facts, they won't be able to solve their problems effectively!

These are just two interesting examples of established techniques available to you for unblocking your path, solving a problem you have, or breaking through a logistical block between you and what you want for yourself. There are many more techniques. Find the tools you need to do the job you want done well. Don't give up. Get information and help!

Eliminate Competing Goals

It's important to recognize if you have competing goals. You might say, "I want to live with a partner, and I want to keep 100 percent of my independence," or "I want to be famous, and I want my privacy," or "I want to be rich, but rich people are greedy jerks." Look at your goals and make sure they are all in alignment with your positive vision. If you have competing goals, you are sending mixed messages to yourself and outward, and then the way life tends to work is that if you succeed in one, the other will knock it back. To move cleanly and clearly forward, you'll need to align all your goals with your personal vision and your unique values. Be careful not to include what you think you *should* do or what other people want you to do, as those may easily be competing with your true heart's desire.

Life Happens for You, Not to You

Life can be challenging, but solving challenges makes you stronger and more interesting and gives you experience. There is a powerful concept—that life happens for you, not to you. This brings us back to looking at each event in our lives as a guide and an indicator. Often, problems and obstacles come from unresolved messes. Sometimes patterns keep repeating themselves to let you know the emotional issues are not resolved. As we discussed in chapter 6, cleaning up these messes is not always easy, but it's always worthwhile for opening our paths forward.

The Yin and Yang of Progress

Another concept, *going with the flow*, deserves attention. On the one hand, I am telling you to be active and step around obstacles—but also to go with the flow and accept life as it comes your way, even if it doesn't go the way you want it to. These seem like conflicting concepts, so let me break that down for you.

The difference is recognizing whether the obstacle you are facing is created by past thinking, is fear based or coming from limiting beliefs or doubt, or is simply life redirecting you because something better is on the way. We could say that chemistry was blocking me from becoming a doctor, but instinctively, I knew it was a redirection, rerouting me in a direction better suited to me.

It is necessary to recognize that if something doesn't feel right to you, even if you can't name why, it is important to respect that feeling.

In some cases, it may be difficult to identify or trust our hunches because of childhood circumstances, current inexperience, unfamiliarity, or our mental health, so first steps may just be acknowledging that what is happening doesn't feel good and choosing to take a minute before responding. Our hunches may be intuitive, and we don't have a logical reason. Or perhaps we just don't have enough information. Either way, if it doesn't feel right, accept it isn't right for now.

And by all means, take the time to act on opportunity when life brings you something unexpected that does feel right or good! Maybe it is what you wanted, or maybe it is something great you hadn't even imagined. That is going with the flow of life. Real obstacles need to be evaluated and addressed, but all have solutions. Most obstacles are mirages, not stop signs, and dissolve under scrutiny and when you compare them to your goals and constructive intentions for yourself. Like all the obstacles I wrote about when I first wanted to become a film set photographer! In time, you'll no longer see obstacles as blocks or stop signs; you'll be able to assess them clearly and get to work on resolving them!

Limiting Beliefs

So that we are speaking the same language, *limiting beliefs* are doubts, opinions, convictions, beliefs, and perceptions that we believe are true (for ourselves or others) but actually hold us back. They seem true from our biased or inexperienced perspective, but in fact, they are not law or fact. They don't make us feel good, and they don't empower us. Sometimes they are simply our perspective, and we aren't considering that other perspectives exist. Limiting beliefs often stop us from moving toward what we would love.

For example, in certain cultures, a limiting belief exists that people with some skin colors or genders can't do certain things well. That's ridiculous. We all have talents and potentials that differ, but they are not race or gender specific. There is no correlation between skin color and potential or ability. Whatever you can perfectly imagine, you can strive to create for yourself. With dedication and persistence, you can achieve your goals or something better than if you had stayed on the couch. Many people never meet their potential because of their limiting beliefs. So notice when you have beliefs that are preventing you from achieving your goals. Choose to be your unique, magnificent, authentic self, and you will attract and create success. Open the flow of *you*.

In my high school, there was a girl who I perceived as prettier, more creative, coolly quirky, original, and therefore more exceptional than I felt I was. She had a great boyfriend, her parents' car was way more impressive than our family car, and her family clearly had more money than we did. I admired her immensely and somewhat wistfully. She didn't have to try very hard, and good things came her way. Her energy was lovely! I had to work pretty hard in those days, and some things I wanted never came. But it turned out that she was an anchorless ship adrift at sea. She didn't make her own way; she had never had to. Soon she started dating men who would give her what she wanted, and she lived the good life until those relationships deteriorated, and last time I saw her, she was working in a poorly suited job, and the qualities I'd admired were nowhere in sight.

In the end, although I had to work much harder, I ended up with an amazing life and career—not without ups and downs but great nonetheless. I tell you this to show that it is important to honestly examine your beliefs in the present rather than waiting for hindsight. I didn't need to feel less than her; I was just different. I had my own strengths and excellence. It took me a long, long time to figure that out, because nobody told me. So I'm telling you, recognize your limiting beliefs, your doubts, as you become aware of them, but do not give them power by believing in them. Acknowledge them and go forward with your plans for your amazing life!

Industrialist and inventor Henry Ford is quoted as having said, "If you believe you can, or you believe you can't … you are right."

Limiting beliefs are self-fulfilling. We believe something, and we read it into situations where it isn't true; it's our perspective, not fact.

"I can't" and "I'm not" are powerfully limiting ideas. When you say that, you are effectively telling your conscious and subconscious mind a fact, and your mind will actually work to keep it that way. You will notice things that fulfill that instruction.

Fortunately, "I can" and "I am" are equally powerful. They give the mind the instruction you want it to fulfill. If you catch yourself saying something self-defeating, interrupt yourself and say, "Until now." Then correct yourself and say, "I can and will," do the wonderful things you want to do. After a while, the negative self-talk will diminish and then disappear, which is an important milestone on your path! Celebrate *that* when you notice it!

Compare your obstacles to your wonderful goal, see which holds the most goodwill and well-being, and proceed accordingly.

Here's an example. I have a loving and talented friend who had a really hard time with her teenage son who was abusing drugs and alcohol. On the day she sent him to stay with a group that could help him, and she was sadly sitting in an empty house alone, a call came in inviting her to join a cool art show. That felt wonderful to her. It felt like things were going right for her for a change, and they were! She had bravely attended to one of her messes in a loving and constructive way, and it created space in her life for something wonderful to happen. Coincidence or serendipity? Regardless, what you focus your attention on manifests—becomes real—and what you resist persists until acknowledged and resolved.

Stigmas and Prejudices

Stigmas and prejudices can both be obstacles to personal growth and achieving a life you love. In fact, stigmas and prejudices are limiting beliefs.

A stigma is disgrace or disdain associated with a type of person, circumstance, job, et. For example, one group of people may feel there is a stigma about marrying a different type of person. Someone may feel there is a stigma associated with certain kinds of practices—like yoga or meditation—from a different culture.

Prejudice is finding fault before we even know the individual person or situation. Often, these harsh expectations are learned from our families or cultures, rather than being something we have experienced ourselves. Someone might say that large groups of people—perhaps women, people of color, foreigners, or people who don't attend their church or vote like they do—are idiots, dangerous, or untrustworthy in some way. Someone might insinuate that everyone who does your dream job is insubstantial, not worthy of respect or trust—like "artists are flakey" or "scientists are nerds."

Examine yourself for prejudices you may have been taught or raised with. It's important that you think for yourself and that you retain or develop objectivity. When you're building your dream life, go for what you know or believe to be of value to you personally and do what it takes to get there, no matter what other people think—no matter what prejudices they may have. Explain yourself with confidence, if appropriate, and plan to find people who think the way you do or who know more than you do in an area you love.

Cultural stigmas and the injustices of prejudice may be an interesting topic to discuss with your family and friends. It can be a hot subject, so be willing to listen to understand, not to correct or judge, and if you choose to share your perspective, do so from a place of compassion if you hope to be heard and understood. Be open to discussion. You never know who will learn what that way.

If you know how you feel about a stigma or prejudice, you'll often know who agrees with you. Maybe you and your friends talk about and explore how it affects you or the people you know. Maybe you have more to learn, and you can ask someone you respect what they think. Maybe you can ask someone you know you don't agree with what they think and why—and then choose whether to explain how your view differs. Again, people can get pretty worked up on these subjects if they feel the other person has an opposite viewpoint, so take that into account when listening. Don't fight about it. No one learns anything on a subject during an argument.

Doubts as Obstacles

In fact, a lack of commitment generates obstacles to test your commitment and guide you to clearing up limiting beliefs and messes.

Until you have committed yourself completely to something you would love, you'll probably experience doubt. You may doubt your ability or doubt that something is even possible. For example, "Why was I thinking that I could ever be a professional _____? That was just a dream." When you catch yourself doubting, stop and acknowledge it, and then ask yourself if it is acting as an obstacle to creating the life you want. I'm here to tell you that doubt isn't reality, and it can slow you down if you don't take responsibility, address it, and dissolve it. Don't doubt or wonder—choose. All professionals experience doubt on their way to becoming experienced or acclaimed. Take it in stride and acknowledge it, but don't suspect it is right. It isn't right; it is doubt.

And if you are worrying about *how* you are going to do something, you may also experience doubt. But you can't always know how things will unfold. You can't see the future.

When you are fully committed so that no matter what it takes, you'll get to this idea you love, when you are open and flexible, when you are committed to taking steps and noticing synchronicities, doubt will disappear. That's because when your focus is on the goal, with the understanding that it is in the realm of possibilities, it exists as a real option, and it is your choice to travel the path until it happens.

As author and coach Blaine Bartlett taught in a workshop I attended, "It has already come true; it just hasn't arrived."

Having read this far, you are well on the path and in the process. By recognizing what matters to you and what your goals are, and by taking steps from where you are to get there, you are on the path to the way you would love to live in all areas of your life.

In the previous chapter, we looked at negative self-talk. These thoughts are not truths; they are fears and unkindness. Every time you tell yourself anything negative, you are unnecessarily holding yourself back. Self-doubt and low self-esteem are signals that it is time to address the issues in your life that you consider your problems. They are guides, alerting you to some messes you need to clear up or accept. Blame is unnecessary and creates more negative attention and reinforcement. Start where you are as a clean slate. "I have these problems, and I am resolving each and every one. I accept my differences."

As you address your problems and accept your differences, speak your truth with calm and integrity. It has a different effect than speaking your truth with irritation or in the same negative tone someone is speaking to you in. The first way allows you to be heard, if possible. The second way can contribute to an argument, where you were never heard, even though you spoke. If you want to see the positive results of your truth, start practicing kindly speaking your truth on small things. Build up to the truths that will change your life for the better.

Keep Your Eyes on the Prize

Hold your sights on your wonderful goal and take the next indicated steps in that direction. Be clearly committed to your goal and recognize doubts, fears, and worry as obstacles, as limiting beliefs, not as fact or truth. They are merely flags that something is still unresolved.

Everyone has personal problems, and most people have had trauma in their childhoods to some degree or another. We all started life as clean slates to a great extent, and the blessings and troubles of our childhood have defined who we are—*until now*. Now we are on our paths to healing our personal problems, cleaning up our messes, and opening ourselves up to what we would love to have—*that or something better yet!*

Unblocking the Obstacles in Your Thoughts and Feelings

Journaling is a valuable way of processing blocks and obstacles in our thoughts and emotions. Let's say you are having doubts about your goals or problems motivating yourself to take the next indicated steps in the direction you want to head. Perhaps something is bothering you that you can't put your finger on. If you journal about what you are sensing, your truths will begin to come to you, and your issues will begin to process and release. In her book *Be Your Own Shaman*, author, teacher, and healer Deborah King writes the following:

> To my surprise, one of the simplest tools I found
> in my research for healing turned out to be one of
> the most powerful. I discovered that writing in a
> personal journal gave voice (movement and release)

to the truth about the traumas of my childhood …
in order to have a fulfilling life, complete with a
healthy body and relationships, we have to own our
emotions. They are a natural part of who we are. We
need to experience them fully and then let them go.
In essence, to be truly strong and joyful we have to
live in truth. Journaling helps us do that.

Looking at Wanting, Wishing, Need, and Intention

There is a saying, *be careful of what you wish*—because wishes can
come true. To our minds, wishing is asking. Sincere and repeated
wishing often produces results because we instinctively do what it
takes to satisfy the feeling. Keep your wishes and thoughts to things
that are part of your clear choices and well-being, because both
positive and negative repetitive wishes are self-fulfilling.

Like wishing, *wanting something* feels a certain way; it has a specific
energetic feeling, as does the feeling of *needing*. They signal the brain
to act on behalf of what you want or think you need—be it ice cream
or a type of job.

To see what I mean, right now, think about something you'd
like to eat or drink. Imagine it, warm or cool, savory or sweet and
delicious. Now take a minute and wish for it. Feel wishing. Really
wish you could have some. Now, silently in your mind, want it. Feel
wanting. Want it badly, but it's not here. Now directly state that you
are going to act. State that you are going to go get it or that you are
decidedly not going to go get it. Do you feel the difference?

They are all sending a request signal, but *stating* is more
intentionally clear and direct in creating clear results. Needing,
wishing, and wanting are low-energy feelings. If you want something,

stop *wanting* it and instead *choose* it—choose to have it. Choose to make it be the way you want it. Intend to get it and to have it. Or recognize that it doesn't serve you, choose to let the thought go, and move on. Some people live wishing and hoping things will get better. They wait for the day when ... Other people actively move toward what they want. Stating generates action and results. Know and practice the difference.

Know that intention has power. It has the power to cause decisions to be made and actions to be taken. It's that simple and straightforward.

As much as possible, act intentionally in support of what is good in your life and helpful for your plans. Let yourself be inspired and on fire about your plans and goals. Feel the energetic power in your ideas and intentions!

The Energy of Emotions

In the present, if you feel repetitive negative emotions like fear, sadness, blame, or anger, they can be obstacles to fulfilling your dreams and goals. Recognize them when they arise and then focus on purposefully shifting to a different and positive energetic frequency, as we've discussed. For your long-term plans, it is best to begin doing your personal work now (as we looked at in chapter 6) to heal the repetitive negative reactions so they're released and resolved, gone from your life—leaving a more balanced, centered you.

In the Body Code app, Dr. Bradley Nelson states, "Negative emotions are vibrational frequencies that are generated by your organs and glands in response to stress, a bad experience, a negative thought, or an imbalance in the body ... and are an important part of your internal guidance system." While healthy in appropriate situations, fear and anger are negative emotions, with specific energetic frequencies, and they are literally harmful to your body and mind if retained and reactively repeated. We all know angry people; for them, the ups and downs of life, the things they don't want, inevitably evoke anger or irritation. Not everyone reacts that way, because not everyone has retained and memorized the negative energy frequency of anger. This does not contradict the principle that anger is healthy. A temporary reaction of anger when someone has infringed on your well-being is normal and important, because it is a clue, a guide that something isn't right. However, being reactive, with the memorized energetic frequency of anger getting triggered easily in you, and you becoming offensive by yelling, blaming, and insulting is damaging to you and those around you. We are responsible for our responses.

Fear

Fear is an important emotion to understand. In his Emotion Code app, Dr. Bradley Nelson describes it as "a strongly distressing emotion aroused by impending danger, evil or pain; the threat may be real or imagined."

When a threat is real and immediate, please acknowledge it and do everything in your power and more to remove yourself from that situation. That is an important step toward the life you would love to live. If the threat was real in the past but is not happening in your life today, your body may still carry that energy frequency of fear, which gets triggered when you come into contact with something your subconscious equates with that threatening idea, emotion, concept, event, person, place, or thing. Or you may have fearful thoughts like, *What if a bad thing happens as a result of these changes I am bringing into my life?* That's known as fear-based thinking, and it is fear, not fact.

Whenever you detect fear, stop, acknowledge it, see if you are actually in danger, and if not, then move your thoughts to how good you feel about the personalized life you're bringing in. Fear is different from uneasiness, feeling bad, or sensing something is wrong. At first, it may seem difficult to discern the difference, but do your best to name what you are feeling. Remember, we are not talking about actual danger. We are talking about being fearful, fear-based thinking, usually just because you can't know the details of what is to come. If you are fearful, notice that, journal about it, and, if needed, actively get some help from a mentor or therapist or book on the subject (see both appendixes).

If you feel fearful about a choice you are making, ask yourself, what result are you hoping for? What would you love to come from this? What is good or great about it? How can you use this to be of help to others? Stay with those feelings! Feeling inspired and feeling joy and love will replace the fear, because generally speaking, fear and love don't exist simultaneously in our emotions. So don't dwell on your fears; acknowledge them and dwell on what you want to happen instead.

Again, this is the idea that *what you think about, you bring about.* In her DNA reprogramming course, healing coach Annaliese Reid teaches that the opposite of love is fear (not hate, as many of us have been taught) and that hate is merely a reaction to and a symptom of fear. The feeling of love is generated by the parasympathetic nervous system, while fear and other negative responses are generated by the sympathetic nervous system. The two nervous systems, parasympathetic and sympathetic, cannot function simultaneously. They work as a team but not simultaneously. So if you have gone into alert mode and anxiousness, and you want to relax, think about the good parts of the situation and feel love, gratitude, or compassion to stimulate your ally, the parasympathetic nervous system.

Reid goes further, teaching that repetitive fear inhibits emotional and physical healing, so it is very important to avoid dwelling on these negative reactions and thoughts. Acknowledge your feelings and either journal or talk them through, or purposefully get involved in the solution or a healthy present-moment activity.

If you find you are inclined toward fear-based thinking and emotions, please copy or print out pages 12, 14, and 17 from your ✎*Workbook*. Then, when you start to worry, read them over and over while feeling the joy, until you feel the shift away from past reactivity to a more neutral response. This is a powerful tool for change because it helps your mind understand the importance of these constructive ideas and to create related positive neuron paths and connections.

Resistance to Change

As humans, we have some inner resistance to change in our lives, particularly if it includes something unknown. It's natural, but it is not always constructive. Remember, we don't have to know how things are going to unfold to our advantage; it's *okay* not to know what the future will bring, as long as you are taking positive actions toward what really matters to you.

Be flexible. Don't turn down an interesting opportunity simply because it wasn't what you planned. If you are presented with an opportunity that you know nothing about, do the research to see if it is in alignment with your personal ethics and values. If the situation is healthy and constructive, explore it; take along a friend for moral support to see if you like it. Explore new opportunities as long as they are in alignment with your values. I worked with a man who was afraid to go to Europe because he couldn't imagine what it would be like or how he could cope with language barriers. Having been to Europe myself countless times and having loved it, I thought he would really like it. But he couldn't imagine going alone, taking his family, or going without his family, so he never went. That is a good example of fearing the unknown. Don't reject something just because you can't imagine it; think about the good side and see how you could manage something comfortably. What if my friend had gone to Europe for the first time with an experienced friend, or booked his family a guided educational tour on a subject they were all interested in, maybe with all the arrangements made for them? He never imagined that.

Another technique to use when your fearfulness is triggered or you feel debilitating uncertainty is to suspend your reaction and related actions for three days—with the intention that only then will you decide how you truly feel from a centered place. The goal is to interrupt your fear reaction and consciously replace it with a plan. Later, when you are grounded and centered, you can make a decision on where you stand and what you want to do. Patterns like fear-based thinking can be tough to live with and require commitment to move through, but it can be done. Journal your fears.

What Do Essential Oils, Music, and Pets Have in Common?

Some essential oils have wonderful aromas that communicate directly with the parasympathetic nervous system and with brain glands, such as the hypothalamus, to create the energy frequency of positive feelings. Certain music does the same. Some animals elicit these in us as well. You are not adrift in the sea of your reactions and thoughts. You are the master and creator of your life, and these are tools to help you achieve what you want.

I have a friend who started having anxiety attacks in her young adulthood; it became so problematic that she went to see doctors. The doctors medicated her instead of getting to the bottom of her anxiety and resolving it. As an adult, she still hadn't addressed the core issues that caused her anxiety, and she was living dependent on medication while still experiencing overwhelming negativity and debilitating fear. Yet I watched as she turned the tide and faced that obstacle! She worked purposefully with her doctors and therapists on her issues, did physical exercise in nature, meditated, and found two rescue dogs to care for, and now she is the happiest I have ever seen her! From this day forward, if you have personal problems, commit to getting to the bottom of what is actually wrong. If actual problems are happening in the present, get help (see appendix 1). If the problems are from the past, acknowledge it and do what it takes to transform the memories from triggers to centered, long-term memory in your rearview mirror.

Don't Move to the Back of Your Own Ship

Don't be the one to hold yourself back. I remember in middle school, the kids I thought were interesting went to the back of the bus, and we did things we weren't supposed to do. The conventional kids sat in the front and middle rows—and the same in the classroom. What was I thinking? At that age, rebellion was popular with the kids I found interesting. However, life isn't middle school. I started to look at the older kids in my group, and I realized that where we were headed was not where I wanted to end up. Be your cool self, but don't get in your own way. This is your life; stand at the helm of your ship where you can see the view well and make great personal choices.

From that vantage point, when you deal with people along the way, present yourself the way you want to be seen. Tell people you are training to be what you want to be, or that you *are* what you want to be and are looking for further training. Dress the way you will dress when you are at the top of your game. Get that haircut. When you are on the right path, these choices are fun, and your actions seem exciting or effortless. When you are coming from your vision, doors open to you that you could not have imagined or planned.

If You Aren't Sure

If you don't know whether something would be right for you, then you need more information. Do some research, chat with people you know, see if there is someone experienced you can speak with, and find a podcast or book on the subject. Think of each of your options separately, make a pros and cons list, and imagine yourself fully immersed in each. Be aware of how you feel. Which choice feels better to you?

Many successful people meditate on what they need to consider at the start of every day, as well as every time they need to make a choice, have an interview, make a presentation, and so on. If you meditate, your connection to your intuition will strengthen and guide you well. If not, sit in silence or in nature awhile and ask for the answer to come to you. Then let go of the question, keep your interest on the subject, and watch what unfolds.

Connected prayer works as well—not just saying the words and hoping for a sign but actually connected, direct communication out into the great beyond. While praying, feel grateful and ask for guidance and understanding. *Feel* thankful that you can turn here and ask this, or grateful to be connected. You pick what you are grateful for. Open yourself to Source wisdom for your authentic self. If you associate a stigma or prejudice with anything I just wrote, try suspending it. Simply clear your mind, be open, ask, feel happy about your path and goals, and your decisions about choices will become clearer. If you still don't know, then either you don't have enough information about your options (in which case you need to do more research), or it is not yet the time to make the choice. Additional relevant information or circumstances will be coming to you.

When Your Old Patterns Persist

You are working toward change, and sometimes old habits, friends, and ways of thinking are the most difficult obstacles. If you find yourself slipping back into the old life you felt unhappy with, you have simply slipped out of your vision. It happens, especially in the beginning of setting new goals. Please remember these are your unique personal goals for your wonderful life, done in your style—not what someone else thinks you should do. The goals you set are based on your interests and the things that matter to you. If you feel you are losing sight of your dream, or obstacles from your past are holding you back, please reread your This Matters! list on pages 12 and 17 in the ♣*Workbook*. It's all there, what you need and want to be happy. Just reread it and know that it came from your heart, from the real you, calling to be present. Add to the pages if new things are coming up for you. Look at your calendar for today and go do something differently. If you could do whatever you wanted right now, what would it be? Go do it—or plan it for this weekend! Get out of the past. Get back in and enjoy your vision.

Do you know what a person's *calling* is? It's something they feel drawn to do. They may be born with the talents or ability to do it, or they may be truly interested and persist until they are able. In the next chapter, we will look at what this could be for you, what calls you, what you would do if you could—or might do anyway!

On the inside cover of your ♣Workbook, somewhere, in the right size and color, draw a closed door and then a path around the side of it. And write today's great date.

❦ *W* ❦

❦*Workbook* Exercises for Chapter 7

On page 20 in your ❦*Workbook*, you'll further describe your perfect life. Make sure it is stable and full in all nine areas of your life. Describe each area in as much detail as you can. Enjoy the process of brainstorming, imagining, and writing about it! See yourself there, truly comfortable in all areas of your life, with enough to share with others. This is fulfillment, prosperity, and abundance in every aspect of your life. When you have completed page 20, this is what we will start working toward to build your happy life, so make everything on this page sound wonderful to *you*.

On page 21 in your ❦*Workbook*, list the things that you wish you could fix in your town or anywhere in the world.

On page 22 in your ❦*Workbook*, list the things you love to play at now or would love to learn to do.

On page 23 in your ❦*Workbook*, list the things you love about your life *today*. Please write these off the top of your head now and *then* go back to your Love List on page 16 of the ❦*Workbook* for more ideas. Consider all areas of your life!

Chapter Eight

What Is Your Calling?

Our deepest fear is not that we are inadequate.
Our deepest fear is that we are powerful beyond measure.
It is our light, not our darkness, that most frightens us.
We ask ourselves, who am I to be brilliant,
gorgeous, talented, fabulous?
Actually, who are you not to be? ...
Your playing small does not serve the world.
There is nothing enlightened about shrinking so that
other people won't feel insecure around you ...
And as we let our own light shine, we unconsciously
give other people permission to do the same.
As we are liberated from our own fear, our
presence automatically liberates others.

—Marianne Williamson, *A Return To Love*
(often misattributed to Nelson Mandela)

Each man has his own vocation. The talent is the call.
There is one direction in which all space is open to him.

—Ralph Waldo Emerson (1803–1882)

Life Purpose and Calling = Your Talents and Your Interests

I f you are going to make money to support yourself, you might as well enjoy it.

Many people believe that we each have a life purpose, a sacred calling, the reason we are here. Yet so many people don't know what they would be happy and actualized doing, and often, that mystery leaves them in lives that are not fulfilling. Your calling can be anything that interests and matters to you! And it doesn't matter how simple or complicated your calling is. Not discovering and acting on it can leave you feeling unfulfilled.

The word *vocation* is defined as one's calling, life's work, mission, purpose, niche, and specialty. The American writer Ralph Waldo Emerson wrote about it way back in the 1800s; he knew it was true and important then. Yet today, almost no one is talking about it. No one told me about it. Let's explore how your calling might look as a profession, a career—your satisfying vocation. Your calling can be *anything* that you are interested in and that matters to you, so allow yourself to be creative when imagining what you'd love to do with your life!

Do You Fit in or Stand Out?

At school and in new situations, most of us try to fit in. We want to be liked. We mirror what we see around us. And we are encouraged to do this, because in many cases, it is easiest for the adults in charge. Yet what if each child was encouraged to express their unique differences from the beginning? We are all unique, and it is in this uniqueness that our strengths, talents, and callings lie. Some people love animals, some people are great at solving puzzles, some people love to make things, and some people love people. We are all different, and what matters to us helps define us as individuals. Actively working to support what matters to us and what interests us builds the foundation for a career we can love to be paid to do.

You'll notice that some people already know what they want to spend their free time doing or what they want to do for a living. You might be one of them, or you might not. I wasn't. And yet the subtle clues were always there in my innate interests and abilities.

If you do know what career you want, then simply staying with your vision and being persistent will take you far. And your interests may change. People progress.

If you don't know, don't worry, but do focus on discovering which careers you would consider the most interesting and rewarding.

To do that, understand and honor your unique interests and abilities! Take a look at pages 12, 14, and 15 in your *Workbook* and reread what matters to you and interests you and what you are good at. Add to them if anything else comes to you. See if you can make a connection between your strengths and any jobs or career paths. Take the time to enjoy rereading them and thinking about what you *are* interested in and what matters to you. Your magic is waiting for you there.

Empower to the People

At the time of this writing, Wikipedia defines empowerment this way:

> Empowerment is the degree of autonomy and self-determination in people and in communities. This enables them to represent their interests in a

responsible and self-determined way, acting on their own authority. It is the process of becoming stronger and more confident, especially in controlling one's life and claiming one's rights. Empowerment as action refers both to the process of self-empowerment and to professional support of people, which enables them to overcome their sense of powerlessness and lack of influence, and to recognize and use their resources.

We are working now to develop your self-empowerment, your personal agency. It all comes down to getting to know yourself and giving yourself permission to be your real, amazing self—stronger and more confident. It is about being clear and determined about your vision to discover and live what makes you genuinely happy and fulfilled. Ask yourself again, "How would I love to make this world a kinder, funnier, prettier, safer, healthier, stronger place? How can I help?"

A rising tide lifts all ships. When you develop, you become strong enough to help, and that in turn brings others up as well. When you excel, you give other people an example and permission to do the same.

When you are on the right path, action seems effortless because you are inspired. The world remains the same, but you are different. When you are inspired, you lose track of time, and time flies. And if you feel uncertainty on your path, at least you feel some excitement as well! Keep moving forward. Keep taking small or large steps. Your path will adjust itself to you as long as you are doing your best and purposefully keeping your eyes open for what makes you feel genuinely good inside. Allow inspiration. Take a small but bold step toward a dream. Feel the gentle winds at your back, filling your sails and moving you toward the open horizon.

Inspired Action

Inspired actions are the steps you take when you are coming from your inspired vision, and doors open that you could not have imagined. That is the *how* manifesting. Acting on inspiration means moving forward with your great ideas and seeing where your efforts take you. You are creative, active in your own well-being, empowered, and creating the life you would love to live.

And it is so important to enjoy the process! Keep your goals in mind, yet don't worry or wish you were already there. Wherever you are today, find what you enjoy about it and focus on experiencing that. In fact, today is a step on your path to where you are going, so make it a step to where you want to be. Even if you don't enjoy every step along the way, value your efforts. Value your path. Don't think, *I'll be happy someday when I achieve this*; that is a self-perpetuating concept because *someday* never comes. That is wanting, not intention. Your life is now, not someday.

Enjoy the Process

It is critically important to find what you enjoy, or what matters to you, in everything you do, so enjoy reading this and brainstorming your great career.

No matter what you are doing, focus on the parts that you enjoy, the parts that interest you and matter to you. Know that what you are doing today is already taking you in a direction, so make it the direction you want to go. Believe me, if you spend time hating your job or your school—if you dwell on that—you'll experience more of that. If you are at school, listen, research, educate yourself, find your favorite teacher, and ask extra questions about the subject. If you are in a job, be excellent. See what qualities, duties, and rewards others further up the command chain have that you would like. Find out what it would take to get a promotion and raise and train yourself toward that. Notice who you like and purposefully spend more time with them. No point in working your way up the chain of command with people you dislike. At school or work, find your tribe, your kindred spirits, and enjoy their company.

Imagine Your Options

Imagine an excellent corporation. Its employees range from window washers to chief executive officers. It has a personnel relations department, scientists, an audiovisual department, landscapers, chefs in the commissary—everyone needed to create a complete and sustainable business. Where would you love to work there? Go beyond "I want to be the CEO!" The CEO of *what*? Environmental sustainability, finances, or personnel well-being? What jobs would make you wake up eager to get to work each morning and do the work required all day? What steps would you need to take to get from where you are today into the department or position that interests you most? What training would you need before you could apply?

Another approach is to think about people you admire. What do they do for a living? Would you want to do that yourself or be part of a team that makes it possible?

When you are out and about in your town, keep a list of what you think is cool or inspires you—an organic farmers' market, a gorgeous bridge, a healthy park, a pet store with its own dog park, arborists working on tree-lined streets, a trolley that drives around the whole city, vintage cars, the police department and city hall, and so on. Can you see yourself working at or designing some of the things you see? Remember, your interests are unique, and expressing them is important to your happiness and fulfillment.

Think Outside the Box

My mother, writer Frances Power Weismiller (1919–2012), developed a theory on population and revolution. She studied international history and noticed that when there was an unusually large generation or baby boom (that is, many more children growing up than usual), and those children came of working age, there generally were not enough jobs in place for them. Most economies weren't designed to take in all those extra young people, and governing groups often failed to anticipate the situation or think of constructive adaptations. In those cases, large-scale unemployment created dissatisfaction and unrest, and the young people would revolt and angrily lash out at authority.

Now I wonder, where were the entrepreneurs? Where were the forward-thinking individuals who saw the needs and became the solution, creating jobs where there were none, making and selling products that the new generation needed? What if those young people had been encouraged in their unique talents and interests from the beginning, instead of being raised to strive for a box that wouldn't fit them?

If you ever live where there is high unemployment—not enough jobs for you in the established market—do what you can to stay away from worrying that you're a helpless victim. Find needs among friends' families and in the community and fill them. For example, if it's summer, put up notices about nontoxic weed abatement and fire season weed-whacking, and rent, buy, or borrow the tools as needed. Or if you can cook at home, go to a senior center and put up notices for affordable, healthy home meal delivery. Maybe tutor your favorite subject to young kids in their homes or at a center that will allow it. Steer away from getting bogged down in resentment and anger. Anger blocks appreciation, imagination, gratitude, and happiness; it is never a productive solution. Filling needs in an area that interests you works much better.

Search High and Low

Your next assignment from me—whether you know what career you'd love or not—will be to go online, to your school career center, or to your State Employment Development Center and read the long lists of possible vocations, jobs, and careers. Read every job on every list and imagine yourself doing it. What professions or jobs require your talents and interests? Really visualize yourself working with others doing it. Figure out where it needs to be done. I'll be asking you to write down the ones that interest you most in your Interesting Jobs & Careers List on page 26 in the 🔖*Workbook*, so once you start this, keep track.

Search online for things like "most interesting careers" and "highest-paid trades." Don't just skim the top. Take the time to dig deep; be thorough. Many creative jobs are not listed in traditional job option lists, so just surf the internet and see what all those people do for a living! Also, some people use the word *vocation* to mean trades like welding and hairdressing, as opposed to *your life's work, mission, purpose, niche, and specialty.* Keep searching for lists with diverse professions, including and beyond the basics.

Keep in mind that the people who write those lists don't always understand what it takes to do a particular job, and many occupations have space for a variety of talents and interests. For example, artistic talent might be your superpower for success in jobs like staging houses for sale or designing websites. Growing up, people told my artistically talented sister that visual artists starve, so unfortunately, she was put off and looked for completely different work; nobody told her that artistic talent and good taste are necessary for related jobs, such as interior design, graphic design, window dressing, magazine art direction, occupational therapy, and so on. Similar things apply to other types of creativity. Nobody told her, so I'm telling you now.

Also, temperament influences a good match. Some people are energized by working in a noisy, crowded environment; others are overwhelmed. Some enjoy control, while others go with the flow. Some are naturally patient, and others are less accommodating. Your temperament matters. Look at yourself honestly and question if your attitudes and behavior are coming from your true nature or from unresolved problems. Accept yourself now and improve your social manner if it does not match what you want for yourself.

Where would you love to live? What are your favorite things about the place you live now? Imagine staying in your hometown with your friends and family and creating a business you wish existed already. Or imagine heading to some place wonderful for training and seeing where life takes you. Some careers can only be done in certain locations; you won't find many seafaring marine biology jobs in the middle of the country, but you might find some very interesting related lab work!

Be imaginative and do your research. Some ordinary job names hide fascinating specialties and applications. What if you read the word *scientist* and it meant nothing to you, but then you saw an interview with a medical or environmental scientist that fascinated you because of your interests and what matters to you, and who worked in a region where you'd love to live? Or what if *engineer* could mean working on race car engines or innovative and interesting bridge designs? Keep searching until you find several great resources for career options for inspired people like you.

Would you be willing to train for a vocation and be an entrepreneur, partnering with a like-minded friend or organizing other interested people who you like to start a new business that fulfills your vision or a need in the community that you'd enjoy meeting?

They Want to Pay You to Do What You Love!

When considering careers and planning how you will support yourself, inquire about the hourly wage / salary for the jobs you are interested in. You don't want a miserable job that pays well, and you don't want to work for peanuts unless you have a plan for dealing with that. Most entry-level jobs pay low wages, so initially, some of us have to have roommates and eat at home. But find out what an experienced professional in your field of interest is paid and set that as your goal. Make every effort to keep your costs in line so that your income will be enough to live on, stress-free.

Back to Your Interests

It is important from now on to recognize and nurture your talents and interests. Have you ever been so busy doing something that you lost track of time? There is a clue there! What are you oddly good at for no apparent reason—like baking, figuring out ingredients in a dish, solving riddles, doing math, or hearing music and then playing it back immediately? What interests you so much when it is happening that you automatically pay close attention? Do you have a hobby that you were drawn to naturally? What class at school did you, or do you, look forward to? If money didn't matter, what would you do to help the world? Journal this! Add them to page 15 in the *Workbook*!

Each generation must fix all the problems the previous generations created. Don't follow the path of an exploitative and oblivious industry; get involved in the transition to healthy, sustainable living for yourself and generations to come! And don't lose time blaming others for the problems that exist. Whether because of greed or ignorance, it is what it is now. I'm not saying there is no value in holding people accountable, but blame is staying focused on the problem, when working toward positive change is the only sustainable choice for change.

It's Time to Be Interested in You

To build a happy and successful future, you must keep learning about yourself and the aspects of life that interest you. And when you begin to choose your career, your creative and intellectual endeavors, your recreation, and your friends, it must always be with your true interests and values in mind.

I ask you again, who are you deep down inside? What matters to you? Have you been doing the things that you care about? Or have you been doing things that you felt you *should* do because they matter to someone else? Have you noticed that something is missing where you live? What if you started that business? Who needs help? What would be fun and make people happy? If you were in charge of your town or city, what would you do differently that you consider better? Be realistic. If students need help, but you would have to charge them high prices to cover high rent, that might not be a good business plan.

Whatever you love to do, learn more about it. Take a weekend workshop or assist an expert. Be the best at it you can be. A job is what you do for money. A career is what you do for passion. Your talents and your passions are linked; find the connection.

Act with Confidence

Maybe you feel shy about what you are good at or care about. Yet who are you not to shine? When you go looking for work or applying for training or education, if you catch yourself feeling that way, change the subject and take a minute to remember your goals and inspirations. Feel your vision! Good employers will recognize and value your interest and commitment. No matter what you feel inside, act from certainty. Show people what you want them to see in order to get what you want.

I'm not saying you should lie or con. I'm saying put your best self forward even when it isn't easy. I used to be devastated when I had to cold-call potential employers when I was looking for work! I would become anxious, shy, awkward, and filled with self-doubt. And when they declined, I would often cry after I hung up. But I made myself do it, and I spoke with confidence until I hung up the phone. If I called a hundred people, I would get only one or two interviews, but when I interviewed, I often got the job because they wanted to hire someone as cheerful and committed as I am. Now I can cold-call in my sleep. I'm a wizard at it! I'm freelance, and now I have experience looking for work. When you are looking for work you want, act as if you are exactly what you want to be—absolutely what they need.

As I've said, in many cases, it is as difficult to get a bad job as it is a good one, so always start with the jobs you would most love to do.

Aim high. If you fall short of your objective, you'll still land higher than if you never tried.

What you have imagined for yourself now exists, because you have created it. You simply haven't gotten there yet. What are your next steps, starting where you are, to get there? Make sure the steps are all written down on page 30 in the ♨*Workbook*!

If You Still Don't Know, It's Okay—You Are on Your Path to Find Out

Having looked at those careers and dreamed those dreams, you may still not know what you want to do to earn money, what a good job or career for you might be, or what you want to do for a living when you grow up. That's okay. It will all come in its own time if you intend to find it. Even if you don't know what you'd feel great about doing, what doesn't feel bad to you? That's a great start!

Brainstorm and write out some ideas on the Interesting Jobs & Careers List on page 26 in your ♨*Workbook*, as prompted below. Have fun with the list. It's like you have to get your car out of the garage and start driving, left or right, whichever seems best to you in the moment! Life responds to your feelings and actions, so head in directions you feel okay about or enjoy, while you are watching what choices develop!

About Your Professional Life

You are your own greatest asset. If today you were personally actualized and fully trained in what interests you, you would be any employer's secret weapon for success, an alpha entrepreneur. You would be at the top of your game, even if your game is raising a happy family, painting for the sheer joy of it, or negotiating preservation of wild land.

Then imagine the next twenty years of your life in a job that is important to you, broken down into periods:

1. Choosing your career and enjoying the training
2. Beginning work in your field of choice, learning on the job
3. Being established in your field and doing great work
4. Becoming a renowned specialist in your field and spending more time with developed or new interests and in the university of life

If you are going to work to support yourself and/or a family, now is your time to discover and train yourself in what interests you, in your field of choice—apprenticeships, education, workshops, finding a mentor, getting life experience, professional training programs, travel, adult education programs, starting a small business, and so on. Invest in your training and personal development. Help yourself meet your potential. Ask your family what support is available for education or while you are in training. Look into student scholarships and student loans from banks. Put money aside from every paycheck. Maybe take on a second job and purposefully set aside those funds for a program you want to do. Research free community programs in your field of interest or the closest thing to it that you can find. And have fun with this stage! If you love photography or carpentry, cooking or problem-solving, find some cool schools or expert mentors and go enjoy spending time learning more and putting tools in your belt. The learning stage can and should be rich and inspiring when you find the right place for you.

Experience, education, and training in what interests you are the best investments of your time and money at this point in your life. They will pay off in the future, and the time will feel well spent, making the process—your life—enjoyable. Even if you are not ambitious for professional success and your goal is to live simply, it is still worthwhile to train and/or educate yourself in the areas and skills that interest you and matter to you. Building a rich, informed, objective, and healthy-minded life is the goal, whatever that looks like to you personally.

And then act on inspiration! Write your great ideas down! Create a plan, a map, a sailing chart with the route to your fulfilling goals. In the next chapter, we'll look at planning, training, and taking indicated steps in the designated direction of your best life.

On the inside cover of your ꭚWorkbook, somewhere, in the right size and color, draw a path with a shining star at the end. And write today's date!

❧*W*❧

❧*Workbook* *Exercises for Chapter 8*

On page 24 of your ❧*Workbook*, you'll write down all the things you can think of that are, or might be, in the way of getting what you want in each area of your life. Make sure to include any personal problems that you feel are blocking you from living the life you want. Add any fears you can think of. This is the place to jot it all down! If you get uncomfortable, try to use your mind instead of your feelings, and then read your Happy List on page 2 of your ❧*Workbook* ASAP!

On page 25 of your ❧*Workbook*, write down three or more initial steps from where you are today toward resolving each obstacle, fear, or problem you listed on page 24.

On page 26 of your ❧*Workbook*, make a list of the jobs and careers that excite you when you read about them or think about doing them. In the days to come, make sure to add to this list every time you think of a new one!

On page 27 of your ❧*Workbook*, make a list of your top three jobs from page 26, and then write the first obvious steps you would have to take to be eligible to apply for those jobs. For example, "Astronomer: save for a good telescope and research schools with astronomy majors." "Parent: find out where family-oriented people hang out." And as you write, see yourself fully enjoying each possible choice! Imagine yourself happy and successful in each career!

Update Your ✎Workbook

Take a quick look at pages 2, 14, and 15 in your ✎*Workbook*. Feel great about them while you read and, having just thought about your calling, add any additional interests you have on page 15, or job ideas that occur to you on page 26.

Review page 11 in your ✎*Workbook* and really feel how good the life you'd love to live is! Having thought about your calling, if needed, perfect or add new statements.

Review page 12 in your ✎*Workbook* and, having thought about your calling, add any additional things that really matter to you.

Chapter Nine

Planning Your Great Life

I want you to set a goal that is so big, and so unbelievable, that when you achieve it you'll know it was only because of what I've taught you. It must require you to grow in order to achieve it.

—Spoken by W. Clement Stone to writer and entrepreneur Jack Canfield

What's the Plan?

While you may not be in control of your schedule and circumstances today, you are now, and will be, responsible for and in charge of your happiness and fulfilling life.

Remember that a happy life looks different for everyone, so we have been building on what that looks like for you. Some people have complicated professional goals. Some people crave a simple life surrounded by friends and family. Other people want to climb mountains in foreign countries. It is critical that you honor and enjoy your own path and goals, not worrying about the goals of others, even if they get more attention than you or yours. The destination is your personal happiness, whatever form that takes.

This chapter is about getting there from here, starting where you are, with focused planning for what you would actually love to do, be, and have.

You Are in Charge of Yourself

Always remember that to one degree or another, you are responsible for everything in your life. Even if you didn't create something, you are responsible now for your reactions and responses to it. The sooner you take responsibility for your thoughts, reactions, and actions in your life, the sooner you will make the choices that bring more of what you want.

I'm not suggesting that the world revolves around you. When you are at your family home, your parents run the house; in school, it's the teachers and administrators; on teams, it's the coach; at work, it's your boss. But like a sailor on a choppy sea, there are things you can do to steer your boat into calmer waters. How do you get along with your family? How much are you getting from your school? Do you like your boss? Will you be a good boss yourself one day? Those are the areas you are responsible for now. Those things are in your control now because you can always be kind, centered, and clear about your position, even in the face of adversity, and you can start looking for where you can go next that is a good fit for you.

In Support of Education and Training

If you are in high school, unless you have other clear plans, start honestly looking for a great college, trade school, or apprenticeship where you would feel good and that would be a great fit for you. Time dedicated to learning and training can be a golden period in your life when you can absorb information and skills that aren't available otherwise. These can make you a richer person and a better employee or employer. They make you an interesting friend to interesting people. Start looking and engage in your options for growth. Find out what they require for admission and start to become that. If your parents want you to be an accountant in their family business, and you want to conduct an orchestra, consider majoring in one and minoring in the other, and plan to make a choice for yourself in your junior year of college. Or do both! In that situation, you are part of a family team, and that is important; at the same time, this is your life, your shot at making a difference, so ultimately you must honor your own interests and choices while respectfully communicating with others involved.

What Do You Really Want in Your Life?

Your work is to get clear on what would make you happy. If you don't know the answer, then your job is still to expose yourself to as many choices as you possibly can until you can identify the ones that feel good to you. It is fine not to know, as long as you are on the path to finding out. Not knowing now but being open to what you'll learn in the future is legitimate and constructive.

Indecision Brings Mixed Results

Here's another thing that no one told me: mixed messages in your mind will bring mixed returns. Indecision brings mixed results.

If you do something that earns you some money and you are happy about it, but then you worry that you are being greedy, money will not flow your way easily because you have sent out conflicting instructions to your subconscious mind, the quantum field, Providence, Source. A rule of thumb is that if something makes you genuinely happy, it is good. Leave it at that! As we've discussed, worrying is a low-frequency energy and is not the same as evaluation or brainstorming solutions. If you are thinking that maybe you might want one thing, but then again maybe you should choose the other, you are sending two distinct signals to your subconscious mind, and what will come up in your path will also be inconclusive until you choose and commit, or decide firmly to get more information.

Commitment Generates Relevant Results

When you are experiencing indecision or doubt, in most cases, the truth is that you do not have enough information, or you are considering outside pressures that are in conflict with your unique values, or you have not committed to your clear objective. It's okay to not know something, but if you find yourself swinging back and forth, slow down and hold the intention to be calm and get more information. In every situation that arises, or in private journaling, purposefully state your truth and perspective in your own words. Instead of saying and feeling "I don't know, I can't decide," commit to "I don't know yet. I am finding out," or say to yourself, "I haven't decided, so for now, I am working toward more than one objective. Either I will do both, or my choice will become clear in time."

Going Forward from Here

So far, we have set up some concrete ideas and processes to support achieving your goals. Now is when the fun starts! This is where you begin to firmly plant the seeds of your future—"these goals or something even better."

For now and for the sake of this work, pick three goals from any area of your life, and at the end of this chapter in your ☙*Workbook* page 28, we will chart the steps toward making them real! Take this moment to dream big, personal dreams. Believe in your potential. Take this moment to shine. If money didn't matter, and you could literally do anything that felt amazing, important, and valuable, what would it be?

Reread page 2 in your ☙*Workbook* about what you love in life and add to it if anything more comes to you.

How will you feel when you achieve your goals? Feel the happiness and excitement of each! Feel grateful that you get to live your dreams! It is so great that each of these things is on its way! It's important to feel it and feel good about it. Feeling happy about something generates the frequency for receiving more of it; it is a positive and clear instruction to your subconscious and to Providence. Feeling good is the frequency for receiving good. It is an incredibly strong instruction to your conscious and unconscious mind, the quantum field and Source energy, that this is what you want and it is good for you. Right now, think of one of your goals and purposefully feel good about it. Feel the feelings. Know your goals are yours as surely as you can know you will go to the next room—somehow—no matter what. It is what you want.

Pages 28 and 29 in your ☙*Workbook* - your Goals lists - will become living documents. Keep adding to them, and as you complete things, check them off or move them to a different folder or *done* list—but if possible, don't delete them. It's important to be able to look back, see your progress, and feel great about it!

If you can assign a date to your goals, do it. That helps lock it in to what is coming and how you will get there. For example, "In one month, I will have a clear, concrete, and descriptive set of goals, in writing, for my fulfilling life," or "Five years from now, I will be living in _____, with my own business of _____," or "The summer after I graduate from college, I will be in _____, climbing Mt. _____ with an experienced group of mountaineering friends."

When you are feeling good about your goals (or anything), you become inspired! Your ideas of what you might do next become inspired, and inspired ideas are important! Going forward, write down and follow through on every inspired idea you have. Take steps toward those goals, research the subject, and make notes of adaptations or new ideas and steps you might take. Inspired ideas and actions feel wonderful, exciting, and interesting. You can lose track of time doing these. Trust your instincts. When you are coming from your vision, when you are authentic, what you are attracted to is on your path. Like attracts like. You can start today—maybe starting with nothing more than your *Workbook*. Holding your fantastic goals in mind, take the first steps.

The goal is to create a crystal-clear blueprint of what you would love to have in your life.

The goal is to be open-minded and flexible about how and what results arrive, and to follow leads that feel good to you along the way.

Believe in your goals. *Feel* yourself knowing that it's what you are going to do. *Feel* sure it is going to happen—that or something better. Visualize and imagine any goal in detail, with colors, people, and places. See yourself happy in it. Feel the happiness and excitement of each goal! Feel actual gratitude that you get to live your dreams. Make time in your days to take the steps, talk about your goals to the right people, and take action. It's like a treasure hunt! And it's okay if you only feel that way when you are thinking about your goals, and then you go back to other parts of your life that have their sets of feelings. Just keep your *Workbook* handy and enjoy goal planning, brainstorming, and active steps whenever you can.

Predominant Thoughts Manifest

Remember, the thoughts you think repeatedly are what dictate the circumstances you are generating. Don't let yourself participate in doubt or fear. Remaining fearful, uncertain, or indecisive generates mixed or undesirable results. As old, negative processes that no longer serve you are coming to an end, if old perspectives pop up, you know what to do! Shift to thoughts from your vision and goals!

In with the New, Dreams Come True

Since you now know that your predominant thoughts are a force generating what happens, which is something most people don't know, your job is to have your predominant thoughts be focused, with certainty that the goals you'll write on pages 28 and 29 in your ◆*Workbook* are on their way! Make sure they are what you actually want. Those or something different but equally good or better. Take preliminary steps from where you are today in those directions. Be open to the related opportunities that come your way. Remember, you don't need to know *how* this is going to happen; you will attract the way. Simply keep your choices in line with what feels right or what doesn't feel wrong.

Now let's look at a few more tools and tips to help you make your plans come true.

Dream Board

A dream board is a wonderful tool for planning what you would love to include in your life. It is a collage you make using words and images (from photographs and magazines) that portray the things you want to have, be, and do in each area of your happy life. Looking at them daily and feeling great about them solidifies their importance and emphasizes that you are calling them in.

Do not underestimate the importance and power of this tool! Behavioral expert and coach John Assaraf tells an amazing story of living in the Midwest, building a dream board, and putting a magazine picture of his dream home on it. As years went by, he moved a few times. He packed his things into boxes and stored them, forgetting the details on his boards. Five years later, in a new home in a different town and state, he unpacked his boxes. To his surprise and amazement, he had purchased and was living in the house pictured on his dream board! At the time, when he clipped it from a magazine, he did not know where the house was or that he would be moving to that town someday. He only knew he genuinely loved the way that house looked and felt to him.

I had something similar happen during Kimberly Hunn's Edgewalker Group International (EGI) workshop in Spain. I participated in Roel Simons's Journal of the Future, where I first imagined helping young people self-actualize and meet their potential. In Journal of the Future, Roel videotape-interviews his clients, imagining that it is five years forward in the future and speaking in the present tense, describing how they feel to have already achieved their most heartfelt goals. I did it, in time I forgot it, and many years later, out of the blue, I was compelled to write this book! It *feels* like an energetic match for me. So create your dream board with complete goodwill and with *your* aspirations! They work!

To build a dream board, take a piece of white cardboard (or use another color you love) and, in some attractive form, write these words on sticky notes: Family, Friends, Creative Projects, Intellectual Interests, Employment, Finances, Contribution, Recreation, and Health. Place the sticky notes creatively across the board until it's the way you want it. Then write the words boldly on the board! Start drawing pictures or clipping and gluing magazine images that represent what you'll love and enjoy in each of these areas of life. Make your board amazing, cool, and beautiful. Use great colors and images. Take specific photos and glue prints on the board. Hang it where you'll see it every day. Look at it and enjoy your plan many times a day!

Creativity in Life

Everybody is creative, which includes you, no matter what your interests are. As we explored, some people are artistically creative, and some people create by making things happen. Either way, you are a creative person who is creating your life. We considered the idea of manifesting in chapter 4, "What Really Matters." Manifestation occurs when what you intend—what you are calling in from life— shows up and becomes actual. That is a form of creating. So on your path, as things start showing up that could contribute to your goals, recognize them as what you called in. It is important to accept and explore them if they feel right, or at least they don't feel wrong. If they keep showing up, but they feel wrong, go back to chapter 6, "Cleaning Up Messes." That feeling is a clue that there is something unresolved and there is more personal work to be done.

Life Shows You Yourself Every Day

It is said that life is a mirror. People, circumstances, and events that arise (and are noticed) are on the energetic frequencies of what you are sending out and calling in. On a busy street, you'll be drawn to notice some people and not others. If you read the news and become depressed, more bad news and events will come into your radar, and people will be drawn to tell you something bad they know about, because you are energetically signaling that these are important. Negative thoughts actually block positive thoughts; you can't have both simultaneously. Negative thoughts attract need, which is not where you want to be coming from. Purposefully shifting your thoughts and feelings is effective. Remain solution oriented and have faith that what you are calling in will develop or finalize when the time is right.

As you start to act, follow up, and take steps on your path, remember to act on inspiration. If something feels so great that it isn't work, if you feel like you could do it all day, if sometimes you even lose track of time while you do it—you are on the right path. That is one way to know it is in your vision!

I love to think about this: literally everything that has ever been invented or created started with someone having a wild idea and then persevering until the outcome. In other words, they had an inspired thought from within their vision and took inspired action to see it through to the end. This is the same process for all successful outcomes; that's how it works. Sure, some people have bad ideas, ideas for low-frequency reasons, or are out of sync with their environment, but we are not talking about that. We are talking about what successful people experience and how we can emulate the way they do things. Every day, ask yourself, "Do my actions mirror what I am asking for and what I want to attract? Is there a mess I can clean up to make room to receive it?"

It Has to Be Believable to You

Here's another fact: each of your goals must be believable to you. Have you fully committed? Do you believe in yourself? Someone can achieve that goal. Can you? Do you have more personal work to do in the area of self-confidence? Remember, this goal is what *you* will love to achieve. It is good for *you*. It is good. Can you please know this much—that you would love it if it happened? If so, then make the commitment that you'll give this 100 percent. Commit that you will persist and then hold steady to the outcome. You will become the dream, the solution.

The Love Exercise

Here is another tool: on your path, in your vision, play the game of love for thirty days. Figure out what aspect you love or value about each thing in your day and just stay with that. Even if you are doing something you don't enjoy, figure out one part of it that you love. Like, maybe you don't enjoy doing the dishes, but while you do it, think about how much you love eating off clean, dry plates. For thirty days (and forever), don't focus on the aspects you don't like so much. Focus on what you appreciate and *feel* the appreciation for it. Appreciation is a state of being; it's a feeling, an energetic frequency. It attracts much good into your life.

Do unto Others and unto You: Respect

Be sure to treat yourself the way you want people to treat you—with love and respect. Everyone is on their own path, and some are struggling. Treat them with respect from a place of knowing what you know now. And remember, healthy self-respect is essential to happiness. Make it a goal and a priority. Feel good about yourself to attract other people feeling good about you too. Enjoy the positives in you. You attract what you think about.

Give but Not to Your Own Detriment

Giving feels good, but self-sacrifice does not make you feel good or bring happiness. Philanthropy does not require sacrifice. If there is enough to share, share it, even if today it's just a smile.

What Looks Bad Could Be Good

If something happens that seems bad—like losing a job—instead of getting into a funk and launching into a bad day, tell yourself, "Well, I'm going to deal with that in a couple of days." Then go forward, responding only to what is actually happening that day. In a day or two, when you are calm, list three or more things that could be good about what happened, like "the commute to that job was too far anyway" and "I'm going to look for a better job and use this free time to organize my garage." Take the charge off of the problem. Remember the idea that life happens *for* you, not to you. Every problem is a guide. What is the solution? Often, when a few days have passed after an event that seemed terrible, when you are calm, the event does not seem so catastrophic. Often, it is a blessing in disguise.

Step by Step by Step

Every goal and every obligation becomes manageable if it is broken down into steps. Suppose your major goal is to preserve tortoises in the wild or to save entire forests. This might include large steps like "get a bachelor's degree in field biology." Then there are the smaller steps you can do where you are today, like "find out where the ten best colleges for field biology are located," because you want to be excited about where you'll live while getting that degree!

To Do or Not to Do?

A to-do list is a place to write calls, errands, research, and other tasks you need to accomplish—often in a little notebook or on your phone. You'll need one to accomplish the smaller or more immediate steps toward your great goals. It's great to put it in one place you feel good about, or you might end up with too many individual notes, reminders, and scraps of paper!

To-do lists are great tools to increase your productivity and help you remember things, prioritize tasks, use allotted time wisely, and improve time management as well as your workflow. Who doesn't want that? Having a to-do list can make things much easier. Your career, studies, and peace of mind improve when you take the steps to stay on top of your dreams, goals, and responsibilities. Start it now! Or do it at the end of the next chapter, on page 34 of your ♣*Workbook*.

Your to-do list will help you make it all happen. What else can you do to get where you want to go, to balance your life and fill it with the things that interest you and matter? In the next chapter, we will look at what makes dreams show up in real life as you do what it takes to build your best life and move in!

On the inside cover of your ♣Workbook, somewhere, in the right size and color, write the word Onward - and today's great date!

❧ *W* ❧

On page 28 of your ❧*Workbook*, begin listing your most important long-term goals and objectives. If you can assign a date to your goals, do it, and write out a description of the great details in each of them. For example, "In one month, I will have a clear, concrete, and descriptive set of goals, in writing, for my happy life." "Five years from now I will be living in _____, with my own business of _____." Or "The summer after I graduate from college, I'll be in _____, sea kayaking with an experienced group of friends."

On page 29 of your ❧*Workbook*, write down at least one important long-term goal and objective for each of the remaining parts of your life. Write your sentences in the present tense. Believe it, *feel* yourself knowing it's what you are going to do. *Feel* sure it is going to happen—that or something better still. Visualize and imagine it in detail, including colors, people, and places. See yourself happy in it. Feel the happiness and excitement of each goal! Feel actual gratitude that you get to live your dreams! Keep the list alive by adding more good ideas as they come to you. Review ❧*Workbook* pages 20 and 23 for what your perfect life looks like. What goals have you written there? Update and revise those pages, or add from them to ❧*Workbook* page 29 if needed.

If any goal on pages 28 and 29 is something you want, but part of you doesn't believe it's possible, examine and journal your doubt now. Write out what you think and feel, what makes sense and what doesn't. Then, using the de Bono Thinking Hats described in chapter 7, break the goals apart. Notice when you *think* something isn't possible or when you *feel* something couldn't work. Journal it out!

On page 30 of your ♫*Workbook*, write down as many steps, large and small, as you can think of now that are necessary to get from where you are today to fulfilling each of the long-term goals you listed on pages 28 and 29 of your ♫*Workbook*.

Chapter Ten

Make It Happen

Those who have the courage to discover and bring
forth their genius break through to unparalleled
heights of productivity and life satisfaction.

—Gay Hendricks, from *The Big Leap*

There are concrete ideas and processes behind achieving your
goals, and there are invisible systems and forces at play in
creating results.

Some people speak of *higher consciousness* and *awareness*, and many
people live their lives without developing these, to no advantage.

You and I are not those people. We do not choose our fears or
our circumstances over our happiness; nor do we close our minds to
our potential. It is important to remember that it's easier to be open-
minded and grow when we are with other people who think that way.
This chapter describes a process of opening your heart and mind and
then goes further into the invisible processes involved in creating and
building your best life.

We will also put what you've read into a catalyzing tool kit,
connecting some ideas and further exploring the remarkable context
of life within which we are working.

Your Ability

Today, you can only do what you can do now.

Please cut yourself some slack, allow yourself to be on the part of your path where you are, and be prepared to take responsibility and do your best going forward. Life is the journey to the goals and beyond! Commitments will open doors for you. It is a fulfilling way to live.

If you want to do more, then you have to raise yourself to a higher degree of ability. In that case, make your commitment to get training in the areas you care about, meeting other people with the same interests and building friendships based on common goals, dreams, and aspirations. Take a minute to put that on your Goals List on page 29 of your ❧*Workbook*, with a first step or two on your To-Do List on page 31 of your ❧*Workbook*.

Manifesting: Making It Happen

When what you want begins to appear in material form, you are beginning to manifest your intentions. You can call it chance, or you can see that you are effective and making it happen, and some things happened first where you couldn't see them—in the quantum energy field—and then as occurrences in your life.

You want the job, you apply, you are accepted. What you want has been manifested as the physical job. It was intentional. That is the opposite of reacting to the mixed results of not knowing what you want and accepting the first thing that comes your way out of need rather than desire. As I've said, to manifest your dreams and goals, *start where you are* and imagine the outcome you want. Figure out the broad strokes of what you'll need to do. Then figure out the concrete steps you can take today to head in that direction; write them down on your To-Do List on page 31 of your ✒*Workbook*, and do them with excitement and pleasure whenever possible. As you do them, the next steps become clear, and you write those down as well.

Unless you are an ultraminimalist, don't throw away your completed steps; keep them so you can look back and feel great about your accomplishments along the way. Accomplishments are manifestations in the process of achieving your goals. You are on your way, and never forget that it is important and wonderful to enjoy the process!

Use Your Dream Board

Your dream board, as described in chapter 9, catalyzes your intentions and receiving what you would love to include in your life. It should be cool and beautiful in your opinion. There is real joy in having all the things you love and want on a single board. The value of visualization powerfully contributes to the invisible process of manifesting. We become what we think about most. Think about what you love doing, what you want. Enjoy looking at your dream board often.

The Hour of Power

Many successful people take the first hour of their day to prepare themselves to be fully in their vision: twenty minutes to exercise, twenty minutes to meditate or journal, and twenty minutes to eat something nutritious (like a whole-food protein shake with fresh berries, quality yogurt, and organic peanut butter; or free-range eggs with ripe tomatoes and whole-grain bread). The hour of power dials you in and supports you all day. There is no question that this helps tremendously, not as a concept but as a practice. Try it for a week. It feels great.

And this is *not* to cut an hour out of your good night's sleep. Twenty-four hours may not seem like enough time to do everything you need to do, but believe me, if you are burning the candle at both ends, you won't be efficient or excited during the time you allot for your goals and responsibilities. Better to take it easy, ask a bit less of yourself, enjoy it, and do it better than to overextend yourself and work or play when you should be sleeping. Enjoy days off and leave your workdays for setting up the payoff of what you will love down the road. If you need more free time, then block some off in your calendar!

The Science behind the Unseen

Understand that the natural laws of our planet affect people on a largely unseen level until the results show up as tangible items or occurrences in our lives.

Scientists Niels Bohr (1885–1962) and Max Planck (1858–1947), known as the founding fathers of quantum theory, each received a Nobel Prize in Physics for their research and repeatable experiments with quantum energy. Scientist Albert Einstein is considered the third founder of quantum theory because he described light as discrete quantities of energy, which he named quanta, in his theory of the photoelectric effect, for which he won the 1921 Nobel Prize. Invisible science—not metaphysics or pseudoscience.

Einstein is most famous for his scientific and mathematical genius, yet it turns out that he was also truly innovative regarding human potential and advancement:

The intuitive mind is a sacred gift and the rational mind is a faithful servant. We have created a society that honors the servant and has forgotten the gift.

I am enough of an artist to draw freely upon my imagination. Imagination is more important than knowledge. Knowledge is limited. Imagination encircles the world.

The quantum field is where we are all connected, and it is how we connect to our own personal truth. It is where all fact, wisdom, and potential lies. It is in us, surrounds us, is between us and others, and encircles the world. Like everyone, you are an energy body or life force entity that is simply part of the larger quantum energy field. The whole of wisdom exists everywhere equally; we have only to tap into it. The quantum field holds all possibilities waiting for action, waiting to manifest what humans act with intention to create. So let's make the conscious choice to connect to our own authentic quantum potential for good and happiness.

Remember, no human-made thing existed in the material world before it was imagined and then invented. Just like the car and internet, there was a time in our history when what you now consider commonplace didn't exist and had never been imagined by anybody. What if *you* bring into existence something people need but don't have—a service, tool, an activity or experience, maybe something that doesn't exist now or exists somewhere in the world but not in your community? Exercise your ability to create and imagine in all areas of life, as we explored in chapter 5, "Keeping It All in Balance." There are needs waiting to be filled. You are creative, so create things that matter to you and interest you. Start imagining what you would do differently and better.

Now is the time to develop and strengthen your awareness of that connection. We have seen how disconnected people function. They feel estranged or exert force instead of acting benevolently from personal intention. Instead, let's make the conscious choice to connect to our authentic potential and truths for the well-being of all involved.

To connect to the quantum field and source energy, you can use words or simply hold still with a quiet mind and open your awareness to the highest, purest energy of good and positive potential. It's invisible, and it's hard to describe with words; it's a knowing and a purposeful connection. When you try it, if you practice, you will experience it for yourself.

Healing on All Levels

By now, I hope you understand how important it is to be on the path of your own healing. There is no one I know of who could not benefit from emotional, psychological, and physical healing and health. Yet the number of people who accept, repress, deny, and put off facing their problems is astonishing.

In many places, there are negative ideas—stigmas—about psychological therapy, as if cool, good, or normal people don't need it and should have nothing to do with it. There are sociocultural norms of acting like everything is fine while burying the ongoing problems. An enormous percentage of alcoholics and drug abusers are self-medicating their problems and enduring them without facing the actual issues and healing past the problems. At the same time, there are courageous people who have endured terrible abuse in their lives, have done the work to face it and put it solidly in the past, and now

have centered and rewarding present-day lives! That is what I want
for you, regardless of where you are starting from today. It's doable,
and no one can do it but you. Know that the emotional stability and
grounded contentment at the other end of the work is truly gratifying
and freeing!

And isn't that what you want for yourself? Why wouldn't you
take the time to find the right methods of healing and be on your
path today to restoring or allowing your wiser authentic self? Every
symptom is a guide. Every repeating negative thought and emotion
is a clue. If you haven't done it already, make sure you read through
appendix 1 of healing resources and modalities at the end of this book.
Use your intuition or interest to pick a few that make sense to you. If
desired, put finding out about sessions on your To-Do List on page 31
of your *Workbook*. Living creatures are designed to heal; it is in our
DNA and in our energetic blueprints. All you have to do is intend to
heal, be persistent, take the next indicated steps in the direction you
want to go, and *stay the course*. The rest will fall into place. I know
you've got this!

Forces Greater Than Our Circumstances

Your circumstances are not fixed facts; they are simply the
outcomes of all the situations you have encountered leading up to
today.

There are powers greater than our circumstances at work in life.
If you want to change your circumstances—as we looked at in chapter
3, "If You Had a Magic Wand"—purposefully add additional positive
experiences into your days. You can change your circumstances to
match your interests and values. You can react to life's situations with
maturity, stability, objectivity, and an eye for improvement, knowing

that goodness, love, intention, and authentic purpose have innate powers to change circumstances. That is a fact of life.

And don't play small. Don't move to the back of your own bus and watch life go by. This is your life. It's been given to you—to unique you. So step toward the things that make you genuinely happy, that are meaningful to you and help others along their life paths.

Synchronicity, Coincidence, Passion, and Inspiration

Follow leads brought by synchronicity and seeming coincidence. Some things that seem like a coincidence are more than that. Act on inspired ideas. Trust your authentic passions.

Here's an example. I was at work one day, doing my film set photography job, my original inspired career. An important young film director came to visit our renown director, and I photographed the two men speaking enthusiastically and passionately about their projects. Later in the day, casually, I looked up the visitor's résumé online. I knew his name—he's famous—but I wasn't familiar with his whole body of work. The first thing I saw was that he was in development on a film in Europe on a WWII subject that was parallel to a book my father had written—which I was just then working on republishing with my sister. It *felt* like an uncanny coincidence!

Just then, I glanced up, and across the room, the men were saying goodbye, and the visitor walked away. If I had looked up thirty seconds later, or a minute before, I would not have seen that he was leaving. In that instant (and not before), I was inspired to go meet him. I caught up to him outside and cheerfully and politely introduced myself. I told him my poet father Edward Weismiller had been in American Intelligence (the OSS) in France in WWII and that I would love to work on his upcoming project. He was interested and comfortable, and we had a nice, respectfully brief exchange. I went back to work feeling inspired. His film is still in development now, and I may or may not ever work on it, but I'm telling the story here as an example of acting on inspired ideas and following synchronicities.

Synchronicities are not random. They are life threads aligning. They happen when the signal you are putting out matches the signal or energy frequency of another person, situation, or circumstance. Follow all synchronicities and coincidences that feel good to you. The right one at the right time will open a door, and you can never predict when that will take place. That is the process of *how* this happens in action. That is the process of manifestation. Your silence or inaction in these situations cannot open doors. Your feelings of genuine interest, happiness, and excitement are your clues for what to act on.

Here's another example: That same renowned film director won best picture and best director at the Golden Globes the following year for that film I was working on. I was watching from home. In his acceptance speech, that director said from his heart, "It's not easy to be a kid," and suddenly the chills of synchronicity ran through my body. I had been writing this book while working on that movie, with that exact concept in my heart and mind, without making the connection about the parallel subjects! That director certainly created his own life. I did. You can too!

Increase Your Resources and Abilities

Another method for reaching your goals and creating your happy life is to increase your resources. Take a workshop led by someone in the field that interests you and put it on your résumé. Find a tutor. Find a local expert in your field of choice and take them out to lunch. Ask them the best way they can see for you to get where you want to go. What would they do again in their training? What would they do differently? After your meeting, update your To-Do List on page 31 of your ♣*Workbook* accordingly. Find a mentor—someone who does what you want to do, responds to your enthusiasm, and will be available for advice as you go through your steps toward achieving your goals. You will be surprised at the positive results when you ask with positive interest!

Find someone you can tell what you are doing and going through step by step; it's called having an accountability partner. Share your goals and check in daily or weekly so that you are accountable, staying focused, and not doing everything alone. Believe me, it really helps!

Ask for Help

Maybe you feel you don't need help.

Seeking and accepting help comes from strength, not weakness, as the stigma and limiting belief suggest. Everyone can benefit from it, and life is better when we are involved in helpful and supportive relationships. People will benefit from your help and companionship. Allow yourself to benefit from theirs. Simply put,

> It will be SO much easier to build the amazing life you envisioned once you're surrounded with an inspiring community, plugged into a structure of consistent support and guided by the leadership of a successful mentor. (Mary Morrissey, from her blog https://www.bravethinkinginstitute.com/blog)

Ask for help getting to where you want to be. Ask for help from your family to create a place in your home where you can study quietly. Ask a business for a job to help support you while you are training to climb a mountain, save a river, or enrich agricultural land. Ask for help from people, and tell them what you are working to achieve. Let them share your excitement and dedication. Ask for help from the infinite. There is power in connecting to the quantum source and asking for help. This tool has been largely lost in today's society and is often confused with religion and dogma, but it's worth recognizing it for what it is on the deepest level—connection to the source and energy flow of life, which you are already part of, the something out there, the unseen universal field.

Get in the habit of asking for what you want. In response, people will either say yes or no, and you proceed accordingly, including persisting in finding the person who understands and says yes!

Affirmations

Affirmations are positive, transformational statements that you tell yourself daily. They are a powerful way to create new paths in your thinking, which in turn will cause you to have new reactions and observations and empower your shift toward where you most want to go. They must be personal, and they must resonate with you. They must speak to your healing and to what you want to surround yourself with or bring into your life. You read and feel them daily. You can go online and find affirmations on any subject, and it's best to create your own.

I was taught to use affirmations on their own, to reinforce and acknowledge intention. My sister was taught that affirmations can also be created to neutralize destructive beliefs and that sometimes they tend to feel unreal when you start using them. Like repeating "I am enough." In that case, to make them effective, you read or write the affirmation, and then you journal your reaction. Over time, as the affirmation neutralizes the destructive belief, your reactions change from skepticism to acceptance and even to satisfaction.

The list of affirmations below is taken from books I've read and workshops and mastermind groups I've attended. I have mine set into my smartphone as reminders that come up at different times during the day. When I see them, I stop, read them, and feel them. I update them as I change. Here are some I find empowering:

- I have a clear vision for my life: this or something better yet.
- I am an energetic match for what I am calling in.
- Money comes easily and frequently to me.
- Life is taking place all at once in the present.
- Today I will make this a peaceful, joyful, loving world.[1]
- I am not the body, I am not even the mind, I am the consciousness.[2]
- I am filled with loving-kindness. I am well. I am peaceful and at ease. I am happy.[3]
- I am calling for a positive solution to _____ so that when I speak with _____, there is no blame or resentment and a viable solution and outcome become clear to me.
- I allow my intuitions and subconscious mind to speak to me, and things happen how and when they are meant to.

---

[1] Adapted from Sadhguru's online course Inner Engineering https://innerengineering.sadhguru.org/.

[2] Adapted from Sadhguru's online course Inner Engineering.

[3] Adapted from Jack Kornfield's book *A Path with Heart*.

The Book of You

Your ♣*Workbook* is becoming *The Book of You,* a living document of your plans and progress.

Buy yourself a good-looking binder and some sturdy, hole-punched, lined paper. Make sure now that there are at least three sections: *To Do, Goals and Plans,* and *Done.* Photocopy or rewrite pages 28 and 29 of your ♣*Workbook* and include them in the Goals sections of your binder. Reread your Goals and Plans daily. Make a reduced-size photocopy of your dream board and include that in this binder. Add to the binder as the projects progress! Dr. John Demartini has a book like this that is so fat it's unbelievable! And he uses it! It's filled with where he's been, where he's going, reference charts and materials, inspirations, and affirmations—incredible!

Your Words Have Power

Declare yourself to be who you want to be: "I am a poet," "I am a healer," "I'm a naturopathic physician," "I am a winemaker," "I am an environmental repair activist," "I am a chef," "I am a housekeeper," "I am a biologist," "I am an artist," "I am a fiduciary accountant," "I am a professional cyclist," "I am a sought-after drummer," "I am a great parent," "I am a finish carpenter." As we've explored, if felt with confidence and joy, your words have power; they lay down neural pathways that support your future thoughts and actions. If you feel doubt when you say it, write it in your journal and then journal the doubt. Felt with confidence, the words *I am* send a strong message of importance to your conscious and subconscious mind—and to Providence within the invisible system of creating and receiving. Put it in your affirmations.

Your words affect you and those around you. Speak only about what you want, about good things, about wellness. Do not speak unkindly to or about anyone. It is destructive to both you and the listener.

Some people make themselves feel important and cared for by talking about their problems and their illnesses. Please stay away from that trap. Our predominant thoughts and communications are what we are calling in, because they function like instructions to our bodies, minds, and spirits. Keep your focus on a happier, healthier self. Be thankful for your chariot (your body) in any and every shape or form it takes today. Intend to help and improve it if you feel you want to. Intend that you'll have wellness all the way to and through your old age. Your body is built to heal itself when physically possible, so make it possible. Give it the nutrition, sleep, and exercise it needs to be well. Physical symptoms like pain and swelling are messages and guides to problems in need of solutions, including drawing your attention to health mistakes being made.

Do It Nervous or Excited

It is okay to be nervous and unsure; take your positive steps anyway. Many people are afraid of the unknown. Don't respond to the fear by stopping. As we discussed in chapter 6, "Cleaning Up the Messes," if you experience fear, take the time to journal or see a counselor and really dive deep; why is that thing making you feel afraid? Examine which beliefs or limiting beliefs are associated. Are you afraid of failure, of success, of being found out? Then, in the moment you are feeling the fear and it is slowing you down, shift your attention to your intention and allow yourself to get excited about your goal. Get back into your vision of your plans! And don't worry about the ups and downs along the way. That's life. Remember, every down is a guide, and most have a golden takeaway within if you take the time to spot it.

Motivation and Inspiration

Know the difference between motivation and inspiration. There is a saying "motivation wears off, but inspiration is forever". Motivation is great when filled with enthusiasm, but if it begins wearing off, go back to your vision. As often as you need it, reread your declarations on page 29 of your ♣*Workbook*. Update them and add to them.

It is not enough just to list or know your inspired ideas; then they are only in your mind. Take action when inspired and lose track of time in the fun or satisfaction of pursuing your unique interests and abilities!

Act as If You Are Successful

You will be successful. Can you act as if you already are what you want to become? Practice being the new person you are becoming. See yourself succeeding. Imagine the cool furniture you will make, the paintings, the diploma, the award or trophy, the applause, the hugs. What does your haircut look like? How do you dress? Start dressing that way now. Act as if you already are what you will be. You are an electrician, a designer, a parent, a nurse, a United Nations ambassador, a what-you-want.

Act as if you are receiving what you ask for. You are; you just can't see it all yet.

Make Time in Your Calendar

Make time every day, every week, to do activities that interest you, that you enjoy and matter to you. Make time for fun. Make time for quiet time if you need it.

If you wait for free time to do these, your days will probably remain full of reacting to what life throws your way, like errands and favors, and you'll feel too busy to do things for yourself. If you're too busy to do what makes *you* feel good, you may find your hours are actually spent reacting to circumstances that other people create. When you plan your week with time blocked off for what you want to do, your life will begin to shift in that direction. It has to because you are using intention to express your priorities and doing what you plan. If every week you take a class you love, or go to a physical or mental health session, the shift is underway!

Schedule blocks of time to do the things you love to do, the things on page 16 in the *Workbook*. I am an enormous advocate for using your calendar and to-do list, as long as you are also scheduling in your free time. Free time and spontaneously doing what you feel like doing in the moment are critical to happiness. Our hectic society has scheduled out free time, so you need to schedule it in. Maybe it will be your whole weekend, maybe two afternoons a week; whatever it is, protect it as an important priority. You need to leave time for life to bring you the things you are calling in, including fun, happiness, and contentment.

Make time for what you like doing, and soon you won't have time for things you don't!

The Purpose and Power of Meditation

Meditation is the practice of quieting the mind and relaxing into the space between our thoughts, into our expanded connection with the greater field. It clears our mind and heart and allows our authentic truths to emerge from under past troubles and autopilot. It is an effective technique for quieting our mind, clearing and balancing.

So many people live with the chattering mind and think that is all there is in life. We tend to listen to it and believe it. But when people like Albert Einstein, Isaac Newton, and Alexander Graham Bell were in the process of discovering, realizing, and creating, they were not listening to their mind chatter; they were in next-level thinking, focus, and understanding. Meditation simply allows us to quiet the chatter and get to the next level. It is also calming and grounding and sets you up for balanced responses to what goes on in your life.

There are stigmas about meditation because it was popularized in India and used by people who practice a yogic way of living. In fact, a religious form was practiced in Europe in the Middle Ages, and meditation is a normal part of many Asian, aboriginal, and native spiritual and philosophical traditions. Many Westerners dismiss it because it seems peculiar, so far outside our modern culture, and they have no exposure to understanding its benefits. Others are concerned because it's practiced by various people with religious views that differ from theirs. Those are great examples of limiting beliefs. Why wouldn't we want to learn from the best of every culture, combine it with our own, and progress in our abilities? Many highly effective people in our culture do meditate! All-time record-breaking tennis pro Rafael Nadal, film director David Lynch, visionary and millionaire Bob Proctor, forward-thinking celebrity and philanthropist Oprah Winfrey, and hundreds more successful people meditate to center and ground themselves and to access their authentic self, next-level thoughts, and connected understanding.

Believe me, until a couple of years ago, I didn't meditate, and I did everything with my will and mind. Since I've started meditating, it is remarkable the grounded calm I feel and the quality of understanding that comes to me when I work after daily meditation.

Please dismiss any negative associations with the idea of meditation that you may have. Everyone can do it; it's an important tool that many people, maybe most people, overlook. Meditation will give you an advantage, and it certainly helps with a racing or chattering mind. See appendix 1 for more information about meditation techniques and options.

A How-To for Prayer and Meditation

The key to both prayer and meditation is to connect. Nobody ever described this to me, so I want to show you something. Read these words in your mind or say them out loud: "what is the most important thing I can do now?" Now, ask yourself *sincerely*, "What is the most important thing I can do now?" Can you feel the difference between reciting it to no one and asking it with connection? Imagine that there is something in life that is greater than you—we can call it Mother Nature—something that you are a part of. Now, connect your awareness to that something vast and ask directly to that greater concept, "What is the most important thing I can do now?" That is the connection of prayer and meditation.

The point is the connection. The intention is not to just say the words and hope for the best but to connect to what you are part of, where all potentials exist, and ask sincerely, "Please help me be clear on what my best choice is." And then let it go and see what comes to you as feeling right. The power is in the connection and in your intention to find what is best.

The Grounding Power of Nature

Another amazing tool you have at your disposal, free of cost in most cases, is the grounding and centering power of the natural world.

Walking and resting in nature makes humans feel good, and it physically brings our energy back in tune with the balanced natural frequencies we require. On a scientific level, the energetic frequencies of the ions in the air at the seaside, the micro-aromas in the forest, the vitamin D from sunshine, the health benefits of drinking clean, living water, the relaxing qualities in nature, the body's connection to the earth's magnetic field—all these and more provide benefits when we walk at the seaside or in the mountains, relax under a tree, swim in and listen to natural waters. Our bodies are made of exactly the same elements and frequencies that are found in nature. Take your shoes off and go barefoot at the park or on the shore to replenish your body's natural magnetic field. When we relax in nature, we recharge our batteries, our mind clears, we feel good, and we can use this as a tool to reduce stress and rebalance and to access and develop our grounded, centered, authentic selves.

The Power of Happiness

Happiness is a feeling, and it is a healing feeling, an energetic frequency with a positive effect on human bodies and spirits. The natural principles of energy are true with television and radio frequencies, with the electrical energy coming into your computer, in the energetic aspect of physical and emotional health and healing, in the quantum field, and with the energetic frequencies of emotions. Everything is energy, and with energy, all you have to do is change the frequency to alter the outcome. Purposefully choose things that make you happy.

As successful entrepreneur John Haglund once said in a workshop I attended, "Inner happiness is the fuel of success." Follow your sense of joy, satisfaction, excitement, and enthusiasm. You deserve to be happy, and if you are happy and functioning well because of it, you can add value to the lives of others as well. No one else has your unique combination of interests and talents; no one has your specific radiance.

Know that your joy creates and attracts joy in others. It is an energetic frequency that people respond to by mirroring. When you feel good, you make other people feel good. Share happiness; go make someone else happy. Why do people give flowers? Because they know that people love the beauty and aroma of flowers and that those things make them happy. Plus, receiving a gift makes people happy. People give flowers to create happiness!

So purposefully choose someone today, every day, and share your happiness with them. If you smile at the right people, they will smile back—and even if they don't, they still saw it. They still registered it inside. Share your kindness and happiness, and don't worry about people who don't respond. Maybe you are part of their shift in emotions, even if you can't tell.

Create the Shift

Please remember the five steps to assist change from chapter 2:

1. *Notice it* (the old thinking, behavior, or reaction).
2. *Acknowledge it* (the old thinking, behavior, or reaction).
3. *Replace it* (with the new idea, behavior, or action).
4. *Feel great about that* (the new idea, behavior, or action).
5. *Move on* (with what is happening in the present).

Live Your Life Fully Today

All we actually have is the present. This is your life—now. Life is taking place all at once, all over the world, in the present. We can act today for the results we want in the future, but what is real is the action and the intention now. So please don't exhaust or deprive yourself today, dreaming that someday you won't need to. Instead, attach your values to tasks at hand, notice the best parts of them, and plan on and take steps toward a concrete goal—even if the goal is more free time! The quality of your life is always in how you live in the present.

As an evolving proverb goes (often misattributed to Eleanor Roosevelt), "Yesterday is history. Tomorrow is a mystery. Today is a gift."

Empower Others

Empower and share with others! There is so much effective goodwill in that.

In sports and business competition, loss is intrinsically part of the equation. If someone wins, someone has to lose, so all the people involved experience fear of losing and/or loss. In contrast, if you support the others around you, a spirit of camaraderie and empowerment arises as everyone's position is improved. Everyone has a good game.

Imagine an office job where everyone is competitive, trying to get ahead and stepping on each other on the way up. Believe me, it happens. Now imagine a job where kindred spirits get together to brainstorm and work through obligations or problems as open-minded equals. Which feels better to you? Where do you want to work? You are building your life. You have a choice.

When you are focused on helping people or a cause you feel strongly about, and you feel good, you are using the part of your brain that releases the healthy hormones—dopamine, serotonin, and endorphins—which create a sense of well-being. People who help other people from a sincere place of compassion or personal dedication are happier and more content than those who don't! And in that situation, the more you help, the better it feels. You cause people to smile, and it is contagious!

This doesn't mean selflessly giving to takers, as there is no balance in that. And it doesn't mean giving to others when you are in need. This means acting with integrity—even in the magnetic presence of selfish competition. Support others and seek out like-minded people, kindred spirits, and people who respond to your authenticity and respond in kind.

The Concept of Structural Tension

Personal growth occurs at the point where we are challenged but not overwhelmed.

Just like in engineering, that point has *structural tension* with associated attributes.

In his book *The Path of Least Resistance*, author and management consultant Robert Fritz defines psychological structural tension as the relationship between a vision and the current reality. Considering the difference between your current state and your desired state creates tension. This tension is what ultimately determines the path in favor of the vision, as long as you feel good about it! This works if you keep your steps the right size (by your unique standards) in order to avoid feeling overwhelmed.

The most growth and change occurs at the point where you are challenged, just beyond your comfort zone, just beyond familiarity and before overwhelm. This is the point where there is enough tension—between where you are and where you want to be—to generate sufficient energy from excitement, interest, and intention to propel you in the desired direction!

It takes time to get a sense of this place in your personal planning and progress, but it is important to find it if you want change to progress more quickly. If you play life too safely and live to repeat small routines, that is what you'll end up with. If you can imagine how you would love your life to be and take bold steps in that direction, you will bring that into being.

For our purposes, structural tension means that if you want to go farther or faster, you have to push yourself into the next unknown area of your positive vision, come to understand it, and step forward toward the next unknown again—always avoiding pushing to the point of overwhelm.

Trust Your Intuition

> The reason you have a hard time trusting your intuition is because you are still convinced that some outside authority knows better than you. (Sufi Priestess Maryam Hasnaa)

We all have intuition. It's not random; it's universal. It's normal. It's just that like so many abilities, if you don't use it, you lose it—but not entirely. It's innate. It's still accessible if you connect to it. And you can work to strengthen and develop it.

Have you felt a hunch or knowing feeling? Everyone has a sense of intuition. Unfortunately, in most modern societies, listening to it is a learned skill.

When you have to make a choice, ask yourself which *feels* best to you before making a decision. For the moment, let go of your rational concerns about what you *should* do or what someone else thinks is right; that is not what you are evaluating at this time. Which *feels* right to you? What strikes you as an interesting option? And which choice feels like there is an invisible block or wall or feels off somehow?

Practice choosing what feels right to you, starting with small decisions first. Get used to it. When looking at choices, act on what feels like the easy, right step toward what you want.

Follow your hunches. If you don't feel like doing something, even if you aren't sure why, think twice before acting. Examine why you don't want to. Is it a limiting belief or a fear that is stopping you, or is there just something about it that you can't put your finger on, but it doesn't feel right? Trust your instincts. Journal your concerns.

And if something feels great on a deeper, authentic level, give it a try! I'm not talking about what flatters you or strokes your ego but what genuinely feels good or right to you.

When faced with choices and decisions, stay with what seems good, what feels right—or, at the very least, what doesn't feel wrong. Trust yourself; your authenticity is connected to your truth. Let's say you have to decide between following a friend's advice and doing what makes sense to you. Imagine yourself acting on their advice. Maybe say the words out loud that you would have to say. Now imagine your way; say those words. Which one seems most effective? Which one seems constructive? Or does one feel off-putting somehow? If you can't tell which seems best, can you figure out which seems worse?

Not knowing what to do or what you want can leave you feeling helpless and confused. When you are at a crossroads and need to evaluate choices and make decisions, try breaking the problem down into bite-sized pieces. Get more information.

And it's okay if, knowing more, you still can't decide. You won't always know. When that happens, trust that you don't have all the information you need to make a decision, that there will be more information on the way for your consideration. When it is time to decide, you'll know what you want to do—or, at the very least, what you *don't want* becomes clearer. Then you choose what *feels* right to you at that time, with the information you have at the time, and run with it. Do the best you can with what you've got.

Have Confidence

Have faith that you will receive what you are calling in.

Noted literary humorist, comic lecturer, and columnist Prentice Mulford (1834–1891) coined the term *law of attraction* for this phenomenon. He was also instrumental in the popular philosophy called New Thought, along with other important writers, including Ralph Waldo Emerson (1803–1882). I recently learned that the New Thought movement of the late 1800s held that Infinite Intelligence (what some people call God) is everywhere, spirit is the essence of living things, including the human self, divine thought is a force for good, sickness originates from unresolved negative mental states, and right thinking has a healing effect. Sound familiar? It was as true then as it is now, yet I had never heard about it until I started researching the law of attraction!

Remember, something will occur if you do nothing, or live your days just reacting, so know too that you will receive much of what you strive for if you persist in your vision with purposeful action! Have confidence and faith that the good you are calling in has an energetic frequency that is magnetic.

The Law of Attraction at Work

The law of attraction states that *like attracts like.* Expressed anger stimulates angry or fearful reactions, not smiles. Smiles attract smiles and joyful reactions of good feelings.

Interestingly and importantly, the law of attraction doesn't differentiate between good or bad; it simply responds to dominant thoughts. Back to the idea of saying, "I don't want to be late," versus saying, "I want to be on time." If you are focused on *not wanting* and *being late*, the dominant thoughts are about *late*. Lateness and stress are the energetic frequencies being experienced and projected, and they will attract their likes.

Worrying about being late causes a stress reaction, and then you are much more likely to run into more delays than if you were to focus easily on wanting to be on time, accepting traffic being as it is, imagining a good parking place, and so on. Whatever thoughts persist in your mind, that is what you are attracting. So don't allow yourself to remain upset about things you can't control. Instead, shift your energy and attention to what you care about, or think about improving the situation.

In the process of making your dreams a reality, imagine the life you want with all the good feelings that go along with that, act on inspiration, and you will attract people and situations conducive to the same!

Stick to Your Plan

"Stay the course" is a sailing instruction to keep a constant, unaltering course while navigating the open sea (which has no roads or turn signs).

Like a sailor, you have started a plan for yourself for which there is no clear, established path. There will be times when the path is unclear, and when compared to your present point, your goals may feel impossible. You may doubt yourself or your ideas. It happens to all of us.

When it does, *stay the course*. If you persist, if you act as if, if you do what it takes to stay in your vision, enjoy the present, take inspired action, and follow through with next possible steps, you will bring into being a life full of the things that make you happy while supporting others and the planet.

You are creative. You are creating your life for the best, and that will affect us all. In honoring what matters to you, you are part of the solution to the problems of our times.

Make Your To-Do List Inspiring!

Your to-do list is your list of next indicated action steps. Let it be exciting to read as you plan and get closer to your goals and take actions in your vision. These are the steps to making your dreams come true. Get excited about that. So instead of writing, "Look for work," write "Monday, make three job-search visits to the most interesting businesses close to horse stables!"

Sometimes a to-do list can feel like an obligation list rather than inspiration. Even if the steps are just logistical, remember that they are directly linked to your interests, values, and what matters to you. Stay in your vision and feel good about the steps you are laying out to get where you want to go. And read them that way!

This Has Always Been True

If you have noticed the dates when Einstein, Jung, Planck, Tesla, Mulford, and Emerson lived, you'll see that much of the information that I'm sharing is not new, and still, no one ever told me any of it when I was young, or until I started looking for it.

I had to go searching for it. When I started searching for ideas outside the mainstream, for ideas about a happy, fulfilled, and inspired life, I was not even aware that most of the people I've quoted or referred to had those perspectives in addition to what they were famous for. I didn't know what I'd find, but I knew, intuitively, that there was more out there than I could see before me, more than I was taught at school or home. When I started to uncover ideas for reaching goals and working out problems, so much of it made perfect sense, and I started finding successful people who spoke in these terms. I have quoted them whenever possible.

In 1854, in his book *Walden*, Henry David Thoreau beautifully put it this way:

> If one advances confidently in the direction of his dreams, and endeavors to live the life which he has imagined, he will meet with a success unexpected in common hours. He will put some things behind, will pass an invisible boundary; new, universal, and more liberal laws will begin to establish themselves around and within him; or the old laws be expanded, and interpreted in his favor in a more liberal sense, and he will live with the license of a higher order of beings.

We have covered so much since you started this book! And imagine your *Workbook*, almost complete, with the big picture becoming clearer and many next steps laid out. In the next chapter, though the end is not in sight (thank goodness!), the direction is shaped and flexible, ready to take you forward from here.

*On the inside cover of your **Workbook**, somewhere, in the right size and color, draw a compass with north at the top and today's great date.*

❧*W*❧

❧*Workbook* *Exercises for Chapter 10*

On page 31 of your ❧*Workbook*, hold your vision for each area of your life and create a to-do list with next indicated action steps in each area of your life, for each of your goals listed on pages 28 and 29 in the ❧*Workbook*.

On page 32 of your ❧*Workbook*, create your positive affirmations for change. For ideas, go back to pages 4 and 5 of the ❧*Workbook*, where you listed what you would change and what you would change it to, and write affirmations out for the ones that are still meaningful for you.

Go back to page 11 of your ❧*Workbook*, where you wrote your full, direct statements of intention, and then on page 32 of the ❧*Workbook*, add these as positive affirmations for change.

Chapter Eleven

Forward from Here

Until one is committed, there is hesitancy, the chance to draw back, always ineffectiveness. Concerning all acts of initiative (and creation), there is one elementary truth, the ignorance of which kills countless ideas and splendid plans: that the moment one definitely commits oneself, then Providence moves too. All sorts of things occur to help one that would never otherwise have occurred. A whole stream of events issues from the decision, raising in one's favor all manner of unforeseen incidents and meetings and material assistance, which no man could have dreamt would have come his way. I have learned a deep respect for one of Goethe's couplets: "Whatever you can do, or dream you can, begin it.
Boldness has genius, power, and magic in it!"

—Scottish mountaineer and writer William Hutchison Murray (1913–1996)

Why are so few people talking about all this? Why aren't these ideas and practices common?

In part, it's because the ideas we have been looking at fall into the realm of the invisible, and there is no tangible way to measure progress. These ideas are where science, philosophy, psychology, business strategy, and spiritual awareness meet. Some of those disciplines have been in conflict with one another for some time, so almost no single group teaches knowledge from all.

For example, if you don't belong to a religion, you might not be exposed to some important information that is true for all people, not just those who believe in God and religious dogmas. Some of the ideas I've presented have been labeled metaphysics and pseudoscience, which carry stigmas. Then certainly, where people were reprimanded or censured for speaking about the sort of ideas I'm sharing, others would stop talking publicly about it. The ideas were drawn from multiple countries, eras, and perspectives, and none of us have the historic and cultural exposure to hear all the diverse wisdoms that exist. Some are business models that creatives don't hear about, and some are creative concepts that business and sciences don't teach. And so on.

There are many reasons why few people are talking about these ideas; even so, they are valuable tools for creating and for purposeful personal development, health, and well-being.

Drawing wisdom and techniques from diverse fields and cultures cultivates open-minded awareness—pioneering a positive direction forward, from where you were when we started together, onward toward your authentic self and a gratifying life filled with the benefits of your choices. If you follow only the ideas we've explored that feel right to you—the ones in keeping with your interests and the areas that matter to you—you are on your way to your happy and fulfilling life! Every journey begins with intention and first steps.

There is a sacred calling in each of our lives to broaden our thinking and work to heal ourselves and the world we live in. Your happiness and well-being are crucial for that.

I often find the words of visionary environmentalist Sadhguru to be inspiring, thought provoking, and valuable. On New Year's Day 2022, he posted this in his app:

> This year, we want to bring together an ecologically and spiritually conscious population to create a massive impact for the benefit of all life on Earth. Join us in creating a Conscious Planet.

I love that way of thinking!

The rest of this chapter includes a few summaries and some last points that no one told me when I was a young adult—and that I don't hear being discussed commonly—to help you stay in your vision as you go forward from where you are today.

Begin to Live the Life You Envision

Imagine where you want to be five years from now. Visualize your goals in all areas of your life, in detail until you can feel it, and begin to act as if those things are already yours and on their way. Make sure they are on your dream board.

You have imagined where you would like to live, what kind of job you'd like, who your friends will be, how you'll dress, and what you will do with your free time. Begin it now. Imagine the perfect society that you would love to live in, one where people are happy doing different things, all supporting one another, feeling good and physically healthy. Make an effort to live that life now, as if it already exists; it does, become your part of it. As you do, you will bring it into existence as you travel along your path. Find the people who think the way you do; if you haven't met them yet, go looking. The time to begin is now, making choices and decisions leading in that direction, starting from where you are today.

Act on Opportunities

As your life starts to grow and evolve, say yes to opportunities that come up that seem interesting, unique, or intriguing to you. Remember, you are responsible for yourself, so follow what feels right. If you get into something that doesn't seem right after all—a job, a roommate, a partner, a college major—you have the power to recognize that it's not right and begin moving forward into something better for you. Look for opportunities to arise, and you will notice them based on your efforts and what you are calling in. When these opportunities come, feel good, grateful, and happy and keep moving within the new situation toward your personal goals for your fulfilling life. You know what they are now because of your *Workbook* writings, or at least you are closer to knowing them than when you started reading this book!

*Becoming Who You Really Are: Healing
Emotional Baggage and Family Patterns*

As I've said, personal work is about becoming who you really are, about rising to your potential. It's about finding your way back to who you were designed to be, to your authentic self, and finding your way forward with the experience and knowledge gained from the pitfalls and inspirations you've experienced along the way. This is about recognizing and admitting where you need to heal, where you are holding sorrow, trauma, blame, shame, stress, or inexperience or fear that you need to address—so that you can be wholly yourself without extra emotional and mental baggage. Working on yourself is vital to happiness and to unbinding your vibrance and power. You have true potential, and when you lead or join with others in your generation, the impact on the world will be tremendous.

The Quantum Field at Play

The unified quantum energy field is where all potential lies, where all yet unimagined systems and inventions are, where truth and wisdom exist in neutrality. It's like an invisible warehouse of everything imaginable and yet to be imagined. People access the quantum field by intentionally connecting their consciousness and awareness to it, allowing the subconscious mind to be connected to the flow of life. Hold dearly to your intentions and what matters to you, take the next indicated steps, call on the quantum wisdom to help you find or create your unique solutions, and open your mind to what unfolds.

Be Aware of Your Thoughts

If you want to change anything in your life, change your thoughts on the subject and open your mind to alternative perspectives. New thoughts bring new results. You can't often change problems by thinking the same way that created them. Attributed respectively to Einstein, Rita Mae Brown, and a 1980 Narcotics Anonymous pamphlet, someone once said, "Insanity is doing the same thing over and over again and expecting different results."

To attract what you want, be aware of what fills your mind and pick good thoughts about every constructive situation you are in. Every day, purposefully go to your dream board and your long-term emotion-charged goals on pages 28 and 29 in your *Workbook*. As often as possible, stay in your vision. What you think about the most now are the seeds you are planting; your current thoughts create actions and reactions, and those create your life.

Hold your thoughts to every situation's highest potential and change your thoughts whenever you catch them slipping into old ruts that you are ready to move beyond.

Remember, when you focus on the things you care about with passion and enthusiasm, it turbocharges this principle. A friend found this on the internet and sent it to me:

> Read this slowly: The Universe responds to your frequency. It doesn't recognize your personal desires, wants or needs. It only understands the frequency at which you are vibrating. If you are vibrating at the frequency of fear, guilt or shame, you are going to attract things of a similar vibration. If you are vibrating at a frequency of love, joy and abundance, you are going to attract things that support that frequency. It's like tuning into a radio station. You have to be tuning into the music you want to listen to, just like you have to be tuned into the energy you want to manifest into your life. Change your mindset, it will change your life.

(Anonymous from the internet)

The Power of Your Feelings

Feelings let us know what we are thinking; good thoughts feel good, and bad thoughts stimulate negative emotional reactions. Feelings tell us what energetic frequency we are emitting and attracting. Good thoughts don't stimulate bad feelings—and vice versa. You can't feel bad and think sustained good thoughts simultaneously. Feel good. It attracts good. It is important to your health and productivity to feel good. Love and gratitude are the highest emotional frequencies that people experience. Any thought + love and/or gratitude = a most magnetic thought. Let yourself love your plans! Let yourself be grateful for this door that has opened on your path. Each time you feel happy or have fun, love it! Love your family, friends, and pets. Love has real power and manifests health and constructive results!

Meditation Quiets the Mind So You Can Hear Yourself

If you haven't already, find a method of meditation that you can relate to and practice for at least twenty minutes every morning before you start your interactive day. When you do, you'll find that your mind quiets, allowing intuition, grounded wisdom and thought to occur throughout the day. Everybody can meditate; nobody has to dress a certain way or join a certain group to do it right. It is an amazing and powerful grounding, centering, and clearing tool. Please have a look at appendix 1 for some types I describe. Look at others available in your community.

When Your Vision Doesn't Fit Your Current Life

There is a pitfall that can trip people up as they are changing and creating change, where doubt enters their minds, and perhaps their dreams and goals don't make sense in the context of their current lives. Do you want to be an electrician in a family of horse trainers? Do you want to stay home in a family of travelers?

Sometimes a person doesn't have support or the encouragement of visible progress, and their unsatisfactory past life ends up calling them back in. The couch looks awfully comfortable. Then change becomes a dream again, just as it might for a budding professional cyclist still living with naysaying couch potatoes. Know that this only means that the shift isn't developed enough yet; it doesn't mean it won't happen. Keep in mind that everything that doesn't feel good is a guide to recognizing what needs to be resolved before you can start living what does feel right. It's reminding you that you need to find or check in with your kindred spirits, your mentor, your accountability partner. This is a process. Stay the course. Journal your discomforts.

If you experience doubt or frustration, purposefully enjoy and get back into your vision; that is what your ❧*Workbook/The Book of You* and your dream board are for. Meditation helps here too, to center you in your personal truth and reconnect you with your intuition and the natural flow of what you are calling in. Then, when you are feeling good, feeling inspired, take the next indicated steps toward fulfilling your goals. In your day-to-day life, make choices based on what makes you feel good. You've got this.

You may run into people who don't relate to your goals and who don't understand your desire for change, because up until now, you've fit perfectly into the life they created for themselves. Some may even be jealous of your enthusiasm and try to put you or your goals down. It happens. If they are true allies, if they really love and support you, they will want for you what you positively want for yourself. But be patient. Maybe they can't see your truth because it isn't theirs—even if they love you. If people don't want the best for you, you can tell, because what they say makes you feel uneasy. In that case, bless their souls, enjoy them as you can, don't believe them, and continue on your path.

Make a Difference

There is not much in life more gratifying than making a difference and helping others to be well. This goes back to the list of what matters to you on page 12 in your 🖋*Workbook*. What if your whole generation joined forces to heal the problems your predecessors created or couldn't solve? What if some percentage of the income generated by your job or business went to a program that solved a problem that matters to you? People who share your views would choose your business before your competitor's for that very reason, increasing your revenue overall while making a difference in your community. That has an impact, and small successes are inherently linked—or can be linked—to aiding similar situations on a greater scale, like creating a local tree-planting group that you link to a national effort to support a balanced climate.

If you are making a difference in an area that matters to you, you'll feel good about it and make friends who share your interests and priorities. Both of those are key elements in a happy, fulfilling life.

Aim for Neptune

This process has been about imaginative thinking and dreaming big. Even if you are calling in plans that are purposefully simple, they are of no less value and are still part of your big dream. Whether it is simple and clean, or dynamic and entrepreneurial, as long as it matches your interests and values, it's golden. Sail for Neptune, the planet farthest away from Earth in our solar system. Aim for your wildest, most wonderful dreams, and if you end up landing on a different planet short of reaching Neptune, know in your heart how much farther you got than if you had never aimed that far or dreamt that big. Don't look at your planet as a failure; look at aiming for Neptune as the necessary goal to get you to you belong.

This Dream or Something Better

When you are in your vision, calling in what you want, connect and think, *I am calling in these plans or something even better.* You are calling in this goal—or something wonderfully right that you have not even imagined yet! This acknowledges that there are wonderful possibilities that we can't even see from where we are standing today. That certainly was true in my case! Doing this leaves us open-minded and flexible, perceptive of synchronicities and the unexpected forms that our dream will take. We can't know in advance all the good that is coming or the way it will come. Good attracts good. The authentic you will make sense to kindred spirits. Help comes from unexpected places. There is an amazing world out there, and there are many ways to go into our own futures.

Create your own affirmation about the best is yet to come. Put it on your dream board and on the inside cover of *The Book of You.* Say it every day in your hour of power. Connect and ask for something like this:

> May I be open to inspiration and providence,
> able to make a difference, available to my vision.
> This or something better yet.

Honor Your Individuality, Unique Perspective, and Interests

You have potential, awareness, and imagination, and the quantum field holds wisdom and all possibilities waiting for action. That is a great combination.

Look for the world's needs and your personal goals and hold your mind on the result. Open your mind and eyes to the steps that will take you forward toward the things that matter to you most.

And as you go forward from here, whatever you undertake, follow your heart, follow your gut instinct, and do everything you do in your unique way. Doing that will take you places you will love to go and will pay off in satisfaction. Putting your heart into your goals ensures that your projects and experiences are gratifying for you, because they match your nature and values as they shape the quality of your life.

You have a combination of special qualities that no one else has, and this makes you unique and valuable. If you are true to your interests, trust them, and apply them, they will ensure richness in your life and pursuits. They will enrich the world as they affect others, who will then go on to affect others still. Apply your unique perspective and find your interests in every project you undertake. Give them each your heart.

Have a Broad Vision

It is important to have an open mind, a global vision, and an historical understanding of your long-term goals. What if the remedy for the world problem that matters to you most already exists in a country you know nothing about, and you spent your life searching for something that exists but just isn't available in your current field of understanding? What if someone like Prentice Mulford or Nikola Tesla created it centuries ago, and no one is teaching it now? What if people who used to do it were considered heretics, so the knowledge was suppressed? We are fortunate to live in a time when more and more information and access are available to us, so have fun learning as much as you can about the things that interest you and matter to you. You are creating a special combination of skills and abilities that will make you a unique human being. Use your unique abilities and broad vision for well-being.

This world, our planet, is a truly remarkable place. It is magnificent, and the greatest problems in it are human made through ignorance and arrogance. Now is the time in history to take the shadows off the truth and to put human skills and knowledge into healing human psyches and this planet we love to live on.

It starts with each one of us taking full responsibility for ourselves and helping those around us in the areas that matter to us. Your generation is so important. Don't follow established paths that lead somewhere you don't want to end up. This is your life. What you do with it and who you become will affect generations to come, one way or another. So as you go along your interesting path, continue to expand your vision and awareness. Open to what life brings!

Life

Do you know what the best and most important thing in the world is? You are alive, and life is ahead of you. Every day is a chance to be involved with what you care about. Conscious life is truly a remarkable experience. And a marvelous truth about this life is that all you need are heartfelt smiles, love, appreciation, joy, care, compassion, and good feelings to bring about more of the same.

When I was in my teens, I went to a live concert in a small outdoor canyon theater at sundown and heard blues musician Taj Mahal sing "Giant Step," a song by Gerry Goffin and Carole King, which became one of my lifelong favorites:

Remember the feeling as a child
When you woke up and morning smiled
It's time, it's time, it's time you felt like that again
There is just no percentage in remembering the past
It's time you learn to live again and love and laugh
Come with me, leave your yesterdays behind,
And take a giant step outside your mind.

Keep your ❧*Workbook*/*The Book of You* with you. Let it be a living document. Add to it and look back at how much you have accomplished and grown, at what you've done and what there's yet to do. Reread the parts you need to, when you need them. You wrote it. It's your truth.

Remember, something is going to happen if you do nothing. So why not do something that matters to you?

We have reached the end of the book! Congratulations! What an achievement you have accomplished! Just think of it. You started where you were and sailed intentionally to where you are today! Keep going to where you dream to be!

If you'd like to stay in touch along the way forward, and I'm around, message me at www.BuildingYourBestLife.net.

Thank you for taking the path to this point with me. You've got this now. May it be a marvelous journey.

*On the inside cover of your ❧Workbook, somewhere, in
a size and color you choose, draw a hashtag and write ~
#I've Got This ~ and today's watershed date.*

Appendix 1

Resources and Healing Modalities

Your beliefs become your thoughts
Your thoughts become your words
Your words become your actions
Your actions become your habits
Your habits become your values
Your values become your destiny

—Mahatma Gandhi

Reader, this is not intended to be a complete list of healing modalities or resources. It's a start, to help you understand the diversity of what exists. Please look locally as well as online to seek out what you need. Some of the modalities listed below are covered by health insurance, others are free, and others are more affordable in a group setting than one-on-one.

Accelerated experiential dynamic psychotherapy (AEDP): Working with a licensed mental health professional trained in this technique, AEDP is an approach for corrective emotional and relational experience to help process overwhelming emotions associated with trauma (https://aedpinstitute.org/about-aedp/).

Acupressure and acupuncture: Alternative, Indian, and Chinese medicine techniques, working with the life energy of the body, energy meridians, and pressure points to clear energy blockages and facilitate healthy energetic flow to restore health.

Applied kinesiology (AK): Commonly known as muscle testing, applied kinesiology is a technique where, by applying pressure to certain muscles while asking a client specific questions, a trained practitioner uses muscle weaknesses and strengths to identify physical conditions, mental perspectives and beliefs, emotional conditions, and responses.

Aromatherapy: Every aroma/smell has an energetic frequency that stimulates the limbic system, a complex system of nerves and networks in the brain, involving several areas dealing with instinct and mood. For example, essential oils are plant oils distilled for their powerful aromas. When essential oils are inhaled through the nose, our olfactory system sends information to our limbic system and the regions of the brain related to emotion and memory. Essential oils are selected and purified for the effect they have on the human body and emotions.

Ayurvedic medicine: A traditional Indian system of medicine and holistic approach to healing disease using diet, herbal compounds, minerals, and relaxation techniques.

Byron Katie's The Work: A systematic approach to personal problems and stress, toward personal wisdom, processing problems, and emotional recovery (https://thework.com/).

Chakra balancing: A form of energy work that focuses on clearing and balancing the chakra energy centers associated with emotional symptoms, nerve bundles, and organs.

Chinese Medicine: See Traditional Chinese Medicine (TCM) below.

Chiropractic body balancing: Works with the skeletal, neural, and muscular systems to restore normal function and balance.

Discover Healing's Emotion Code, Body Code, and Belief Code: These are modalities of energy work that address unresolved emotions, beliefs, and physical symptoms that persist from past experiences, identifying them and releasing the energetic frequencies from the body to restore mental, emotional, and physical health (https://discoverhealing.com/).

DNA reprogramming course by Annaliese Reid: Teaches methods to use the natural healing abilities of the body and mind to restore physical, mental, and emotional health (https://dnareprogramming.online/).

Dream work: Explores the images, stories, and emotions of dreams to decipher what the mind is processing or cycling—with the idea that our unconscious or subconscious mind is attempting to process problems, concerns, and stresses or express concepts.

Emotional Freedom Technique (EFT): This is a mind-body method of tapping specific points on the body (these points are also used in acupuncture and acupressure) when uncomfortable feelings or concerns arise, in order to process and neutralize repetitive negative emotional associations and reactions.

Eye movement desensitization and reprogramming (EMDR): Working with a licensed mental health professional trained in this technique, EMDR involves moving your eyes a specific way while you process traumatic memories and is designed to heal trauma and alleviate distress associated with traumatic memories.

Forest bathing: See "Nature heals" below. A balancing and rejuvenating practice of being in nature that engages the five senses and the meditative capability of the mind and consciousness to tune into the location (forest, park, seaside). The intention is to sense nature and be immersed in the natural energetic frequencies involved in the smells, sounds, tastes (such as beneficial herbs, plants, and minerals), to look purposefully at the visual beauty of uninterrupted natural environments, and to feel the breeze, shade, or sunshine and the tactile sensations of earth, stone, and plants. Doing this syncs the body with the natural frequencies of the planet, which is restorative to humans and all living things.

Grief support groups: These groups are led by individuals trained in providing validation, emotional support, and education about the nature and processing of grief.

Hawaiian Ho'oponopono: A four-step Hawaiian traditional healing practice, effective for individual and relational resolution and forgiveness. Hawaiian healing priestess Morrnah Simeon adapted traditional Ho'oponopono to address modern social situations, and her student Dr. Ihaleakala Hew Len brought it further into the public eye by using it when he worked with the criminally insane (see the book *Zero Limits* in appendix 2).

Health or healing coaches: People trained in healing modalities and techniques who work with individuals and groups to achieve emotional, spiritual, mental, and physical health goals.

HeartMath Institute (including Heart Coherence training): A scientific organization focusing on the psychophysiology of interactions between the heart and brain and innovative approaches to emotional well-being related to healthy heart rhythm patterns and physiological coherence (https://www.heartmath.org/).

Holistic nutritional therapy using diagnostic muscle testing: An approach to the nutritional needs of the body for physical healing, using kinesiological muscle testing to determine nutritional deficits and overages that impact the body's health and healing capabilities.

Inner Engineering by Sadhguru: A system and approach for mental, emotional, spiritual, and physical well-being derived from the science and multilevel principals of yoga (https://innerengineering.sadhguru.org/).

Journaling: The practice of writing down our thoughts, feelings, reactions, fears, and challenging or empowering experiences, and to explore reactions and feelings about stressful life events, with the objective of processing and constructively understanding feelings and reactivity.

Massage: Transformative body massage work is where the practitioner rubs and kneads skin, muscles, tendons, and ligaments to alleviate pain, tension, and stress and to relax and detoxify areas where these are held.

Meditation: There are many techniques. Here are a few:

1. Six-phase meditation by Vishen Lakhiani of Mind Valley: https://www.mindvalley.com/learn-meditation
2. Deborah King's mantra-based meditation: https://deborahking.com/courses/vedic-meditation/
3. Isha-kriya meditation by Sadhguru at the Isha Institute: https://isha.sadhguru.org/in/en/yoga-meditation/yoga-program-for-beginners/isha-kriya-meditation
4. Self-Realization Fellowship meditation: https://onlinemeditation.yogananda.org/
5. Transcendental Meditation: https://www.tm.org/

Mental health–promoting resources:

1. Mindfulness for Teens: https://www.mindfulnessforteens.com/
2. Resources for LGBTQ youth: https://www.thetrevorproject.org/
3. Sexual Abuse National Network (RAINN): https://www.rainn.org/resources
4. Society for Adolescent Health and Medicine (SAHM): https://www.adolescenthealth.org/
5. Substance Abuse and Mental Health Services Administration (SAMHSA): https://www.samhsa.gov/

6. The PsychANP, https://www.psychanp.org/, founded by a group of naturopathic physicians seeking to expand the field of naturopathic mind-body medicine
7. The Youth Mental Health Project: https://ymhproject.org/ and https://ymhproject.org/resources/
8. Young Men's Health: https://youngmenshealthsite.org/
9. Young Women's Health: https://youngwomenshealth.org/

Or contact your local mental health advocates. You can find information though schools, work, churches, or on the internet.

Muscle testing: See "Applied kinesiology (AK)" above.

Music: There is remarkable research about sound and music's effects on our bodies, emotions, and outlook. Sound frequencies move through the water and energy meridians of our bodies, creating effects. Singing and humming create a positive physical vibration in the area near our hearts, thymus, and lungs that stimulates calm and well-being.

Nature heals: See "Forest bathing" above. Research and reports from institutions such as the American Psychological Association and Yale University show how being active or meditative in nature can help with chronic physical symptoms, relieve stress, reduce depression, strengthen the immune system, and promote the body's ability to self-heal through natural physiological functions, such as increased release of dopamine and reduced production or increased processing of stress hormones.

Neuro Emotional Technique (NET): A cognitive, emotional, and behavioral technique to relieve symptoms related to mental, emotional, and physical stress (https://www.netmindbody.com/).

Qigong, exercise and martial art: A traditional practice system using postures, movement, breathing, and meditation for health and spiritual connection, to cultivate qi, and used in martial arts training.

Qigong, medical/healing form: Medical qigong uses specific exercises and consciousness meditations to address and balance the energies of the body, mind, spirit, and emotions toward the goal of integrated well-being and with the idea that imbalance in any area manifests as problems in any and all areas.

Quantum healing: Quantum healing is based on the principles of quantum physics, which indicate that everything in the universe is made up of energy; from intention to exercise, the scientific principles of quantum physics affect physical, mental, and emotional health, and healing can be facilitated using the principles of quantum physics and energy.

Reflexology: Involves application of pressure and massage to specific points on the hands, feet, and ears to stimulate nerve function, increase circulation, release toxins, improve sleep, boost energy, and stimulate healing and recovery from injuries.

Reiki: A Japanese form of energy healing where specific energetic frequencies are directed to the client or patient to stimulate the self-healing ability of the body, energy body, mind, and emotions, causing relaxation and reducing anxiety, tension, and pain.

Shamanic healing: Shamans from different cultures use different traditions, techniques, and modalities to heal others. Many shamans use medicinal plants, prayer, ritual, spiritual journeys, energy field merging, and negative energy clearing through connection to a higher source.

Shiatsu bodywork: A Japanese form of massage and bodywork using pressure points and acupressure to release tension, reduce pain, activate healthy energy in the body, and restore energetic balance to the body.

Sound healing: Uses specific therapeutic tones, music, octaves, instruments, binaural beats, sonic frequencies, and vibrations to stimulate the body's healthy energetic frequencies, reduce stress and tension, activate healthy biochemicals and hormones, balance the body, and support health and healing.

Stress mitigation and management: Recognizing that recurring or ongoing stress and the presence of stress hormones in our bodies is damaging to the physical body, this focuses on relaxation, emotional processing, negative energy release through exercise, and time in nature.

Talk therapy: Psychotherapy with a licensed mental health professional based on talking about one's problems, explaining situations, asking and answering questions of oneself, self-realization and discovery, processing emotions and stresses through communication. It alleviates isolation, allows one to find and develop personal truth, and vents tensions.

Therapy or counseling groups: In addition to the benefits of talk therapy listed above, group therapy offers companionship, different perspectives, and accountability and is often less expensive than one-on-one private practice therapy and counseling.

Traditional Chinese Medicine (TCM): Concepts and treatments developed over centuries in China to address illness and disease, addressing the body as a whole and integrated system using acupuncture, massage, exercise, diet, herbal remedies, and meditation.

Twelve-step groups: There are many different types of twelve-step groups, including substance abuse, harmful behavioral patterns, and relationship challenges. The great thing about these groups is that they stimulate change and are free, found in most communities, really supportive, and anonymous. Go online to read about all the twelve-step options. Then try a few different groups to find your home (https://12step.org/references/12-step-versions/).

Yoga: Yoga is generally thought of as a physical practice of postures and repeated stretches and exercises for physical health, stress reduction, agility, and relaxation. In fact, it is a greater philosophy that includes whole-health efforts, including physical health techniques, spiritual connection and awareness, consciousness and meditation, physical practices involving the five senses and emotions, and principles such as the value of compassion, personal responsibility, and objectivity perspectives.

Appendix 2

Organizations, Individuals, Books, and Podcasts for Well-Being and Forward Thinking

Reader, this is not a comprehensive list, but it includes my favorites, provided here for inspiration. We are not alone in our interests.

Organizations and Individuals of Interest and Importance:

Annaliese S. Reid: DNA reprogramming for physical self-healing, https://dnareprogramming.online/

Brave Thinking Institute, Mary Morrissey, founder: https://www.bravethinkinginstitute.com/

Bruce H. Lipton, PhD: Bridging science and spirit, https://www.brucelipton.com/

Canfield training: Maximizing human potential, https://jackcanfield. com/trainings/

Conscious Planet movement: https://consciousplanet.org/

Deborah King Institute of LifeForce Energy Healing®: https:// deborahking.com/

Demartini Institute: Human behavior specialists, maximizing human awareness and potential, dedicated to expanding human awareness and potential: https://drdemartini.com/

DNA reprogramming for self-healing, Annaliese Reid, founder: https://dnareprogramming.online/

Donna Pace, creative strategist and human design analyst: http:// donnapace.com/

Dr. Glen Rein, quantum biologist: https://quantum-biology.org/

Dr. John F. Demartini, human behavioral specialist, educator, author, CEO, and founder: https://drdemartini.com/

Dr. Masaru Emoto and water consciousness: The Wellness Enterprise, https://thewellnessenterprise.com/emoto/

Edgewalker Group International (EGI), Kimberly Hunn, founder: http://edgewalkergroup.com/

HeartMath Institute: Heart coherence, https://www.heartmath.org/

Isha Foundation and the Inner Engineering program: https://isha.sadhguru.org/us/en

Jack Canfield of the Canfield Training Group: https://jackcanfield.com/

John Kehoe, Finding Your Purpose | Mind Power: https://www.learnmindpower.com/

John Reid: Sound healing, https://cymascope.com/

Journal of the Future, Roel Simons, founder: www.journalofthefuture.com/

Lateral Thinking, Edward de Bono, founder: https://www.debono.com/

MindValley: Online personal transformation learning platform, https://www.mindvalley.com/

The Shift Network: Leaders in personal development webinars, https://theshiftnetwork.com/

Podcasts:

Let's Talk about Mental Health, with host Jeremy Godwin: https://letstalkaboutmentalhealth.com.au/platforms/

The Mel Robbins Podcast, with host Mel Robbins: https://www.melrobbins.com/

The Psychology of Your Twenties, with host Jemma Sbeg: https://podcasts.apple.com/my/podcast/the-psychology-of-your-20s/id1573710078

Books of Interest:

A Mind of Your Own: The Truth about Depression and How Women Can Heal Their Bodies to Reclaim Their Lives by Kelly Brogan, MD

A Path With Heart: A Guide through the Perils and Promises of Spiritual Life by Jack Kornfield

A Return to Love: Reflections on the Principles of "A Course in Miracles" by Marianne Williamson

Brave Thinking: The Art and Science of Creating a Life You Love by Mary Morrissey

Building Your Best Life: A Young Person's Guide to Creating the Life You'd Love to Live by Merie Weismiller Wallace, MFA, CBCP

Compassionate Capitalism: Journey to the Soul of Business by Blaine Bartlett and David Meltzer

Cultivating Qi: The Root of Energy, Vitality, and Spirit by David W. Clippiner

E-Squared: Nine Do-It-Yourself Energy Experiments That Prove Your Thoughts Create Your Reality by Pam Grout

Eat, Pray, Love: One Woman's Search for Everything Across Italy, India, and Indonesia by Elizabeth Gilbert

One Year to an Organized Life: From Your Closets to Your Finances, the Week-by-Week Guide to Getting Completely Organized for Good by Regina Leeds

Personal Finance for Dummies by Eric Tyson

Power vs. Force: The Hidden Determinants of Human Behavior by David R. Hawkins, MD, PhD

Secrets of the Lost Mode of Prayer: The Hidden Power of Beauty, Blessing, Wisdom, and Hurt by Gregg Braden

Six Thinking Hats, Lateral Thinking: A Practical and Uniquely Positive Approach to Making Decisions and Exploring New Ideas by Edward de Bono

Spontaneous Healing of Belief: Shattering the Paradigm of False Limits by Gregg Braden

The Artist's Way: A Spiritual Path to Higher Creativity by Julia Cameron

The Big Leap: Take Life to the Next Level by Gay Hendricks

The Biology of Belief: Unleashing the Power of Consciousness, Matter, and Miracles by Bruce Lipton

The Body Keeps the Score: Brain, Mind, and Body in the Healing of Trauma by Bessel Van Der Kolk, MD

The Emotion Code: How to Release Your Trapped Emotions for Abundant Health, Love, and Happiness by Dr. Bradley Nelson

The Essential Rumi: New Expanded Edition by Jalal al-Din Rumi (author) Coleman Barks (Translator)

The Four Agreements: A Practical Guide to Personal Freedom by Don Miguel Ruiz

The Path of Least Resistance: Learning to Become the Creative Force in Your Own Life by Robert Fritz

The Quantum Universe: (and Why Anything That Can Happen, Does) by Brian Cox and Jeff Forshaw et al.

The Secret by Rhonda Byrne

The Success Principles: How to Get from Where You Are to Where You Want to Be by Jack Canfield

The Synchronicity Key: The Hidden Intelligence Guiding the Universe and You by David Wilcock

The Values Factor: The Secret to Creating an Inspired and Fulfilling Life by Dr. John Demartini

Think and Grow Rich by Napoleon Hill

Thought Is Force: Life, Love, Soul, God by Tamás Lajtner

Zero Limits: The Secret Hawaiian System for Wealth, Health, Peace, and More by Joe Vitale and Ihaleakala Hew Len

About the Author

Author Merie Weismiller Wallace has lived this book. Starting out uncertain and struggling as a young adult, and now writing at a peak in an amazing life and career, this is what Merie wants to share with young people so they are supported in living their own full and gratifying lives.

Known for her still photography work in feature film production, publications, and gallery exhibits, Merie went to high school at the Athenian School in the San Francisco Bay Area—because, after practically failing eighth grade and ending up in Social Adjustment class for being disruptive, she picked up her head and sought a progressive and rigorous academic education. Merie received her BA from Mills College in Oakland, California, where she was unexpectedly student body president her senior year. She received her master of fine arts degree from USC Film School, attending because she wanted to work in a creative and collaborative profession. She has since worked around the world with noted filmmakers, including Clint Eastwood, James Cameron, Alexander Payne, David O. Russell, Greta Gerwig, Sam Raimi, Terrence Malick, and Steven Spielberg. Merie is passionate about the adventurous and collaborative aspects of filmmaking and photography. She works with an eye for the magic in a moment. Please see Merie's www.meriewallace.com

Merie has steamed across the Atlantic and Mediterranean in a passenger ship and traveled in the United States, Mexico, Australia, New Zealand, England, Wales, Scotland, Holland, Spain, France, Italy, Canada, Switzerland, Iceland, Malaysia, and Thailand, some of which was done on the back of her husband's motorcycle. She makes the distinction between traveling and tourism, living in a different culture versus visiting one.

Trained as a certified Emotion Code, Body Code, and Belief Code practitioner, Merie has studied directly with environmentalist Sadhguru, behavioral specialist Dr. John Demartini, motivational coach Jack Canfield, Discover Healing founder Dr. Bradley Nelson, and most recently with LifeForce Energy Healing® founder Deborah King. Please see Merie's www.ReLeaseEnergyWork.com

A lifelong learner who cares about the importance of the complete health of our planet and all its inhabitants, she is interested in how nature and human life work powerfully in the visible and invisible. Please join Merie in supporting the health of what matters to you most.

Please see Merie's www.BuildingYourBestLife.net

Made in United States
Troutdale, OR
12/12/2024

26317806R00171